THE SECRET PF

SECRETS OF PRISON UNCOVERED

Copyright © 2021

Introduction

Thank you for taking an interest in my story and the time to read this book. I kept a prison diary to give other people that may find themselves in my shoes an insight into the unreported world of prison.

I was charged with fraud to which I pleaded Not Guilty; the CPS took the case to trial and I was convicted. I was/am a normal family man, having never even been arrested prior to this event and to find myself now facing a 5 year prison sentence was overwhelmingly daunting, as you'd expect.

I heard all the horror stories of prison; the rapes, beatings, gangs, drugs, violence and it terrified me and no one could prepare you for what was to come or what stories were true or not. This is why I decided to keep a diary of all the events, feelings, politics and the good and bad things that go on inside prison.

Prison is a big, scary and dark place but, as you will read in my book, there is light in the darkest of places and humanity does shine through in the last place you would expect. There's selfishness, charity, brutality, compassion and corruption.

Then there's the other side of prison; the craftiness, ingenuity to survive and pass the time and suppress boredom. There's the heartbreak, from the children that suffer due to their parent being imprisoned, partners that must face life alone now, and family members who are without their loved ones.

I've tried to cover my first hand feelings exactly as I felt them at that moment, all aspects of living in prison, and what it is like for a normal family man whose business activities have landed him in this situation, to now be in a completely alien environment and trying to survive.

Now I am on the other side and have completed my sentence, it is hard to get reintegrated back into society. Being tarnished as an 'Ex-Offender', the community seems to punish those who have already been 'punished' and wonder why the re-offending rate is so high. I also hope this book highlights that not everybody that ends up in prison is a bad egg. People make mistakes, some people shouldn't have ever ended up in prison and some have just lost their way in life. People do need that second chance and support to keep them on the straight and narrow, as prison is not a nice place to end up and is a vicious cycle that some find hard to get out of.

This is self published, Im no Stephen King so may be a little rough around the edges, a bit like prison, but Ive tried my hardest.

Thank you again for taking an interest in this book. I would love to hear your thoughts after you've read it, drop me a message on amazon reviews.

Secret Prisoner.

Characters are real, names have been changed for security and privacy reasons!

Table of Contents

(This is set up to only show Heading 1 so the main chapter headings but not sub headings.)

Introduction

Table of Contents

Legal Notes

Chapter 1. Court Sentencing)

Chapter 2. Prison Arrival

Chapter 3. The Body Odor Was Overwhelming

Chapter 4. Sausage Rolls & Subliminal Messages

Chapter 5. Induction

Chapter 6. Ice Cream Shop For Druggies

Chapter 7. Aladdins Cave of Contraband

Chapter 8. Im a CAT C Prisoner

Chapter 9. Like a scene from Oliver

Chapter 10. One punch cracked his head

Chapter 11. Getting toilet roll is like rocking horse shit

Chapter 12. Pigeon Shit, Mice and Rats

Chapter 13. Throwing Poo

Chapter 14. Get a prison suite upgrade

Chapter 15. Piss tests are degrading

Chapter 16. She went down like a sack of shit

Chapter 17. Im now a CAT D Prisoner

Chapter 18. A Well timed attack

Chapter 19. Christmas in prison

Chapter 20. Im leaving Wandsworth

Chapter 21. Like a 1950s Holiday Camp

Chapter 22. My bullshit got me promoted

Chapter 23. Stabbed in the neck

Chapter 24. OAP Bare knuckle Boxing

Chapter 25. Interviewing a killer

Chapter 26. A Hitman at Ford

Chapter 27. Inducting a Terrorist

Chapter 28. More Deliveries here than Amazon

Chapter 29. Corona Virus

Chapter 30 Prisons Didn't Take COVID Seriously

Chapter 31. The Phantom Shitter

Chapter 32. Ive signed my Early Release

Chapter 33. Im going Home

Chapter 1. (SENTENCING)

It had all boiled down to this moment; 3 and a half years, endless hours of home research, multiple solicitors' meetings, multiple police station questioning, many extended bail dates, the anxiety, stress, mental health, effect on my family, 2 months on trial and 7 days waiting for the jury verdict - this was it!

The judge addressed us in turn; I was first. I positioned myself on the chair, straight posture and trying not to give any emotion away especially for any of the reporters to pick up on.

I braced to take the metaphorical knock out. He muttered some words summing up the 2 months trial in court. The rest was a blur until I heard the words - '5 YEARS CUSTODIAL SENTENCE OF WHICH HE WILL SERVE HALF'. I went numb. It was done. Jay West, my co-defendant was handed down a 3 year sentence. There was nothing more to say or do than stand up and be led out of the door on the right and down to the cells.

I felt like I was drifting, floating down the stairs, not in an ecstasy or happy way but in a complete state of shock; it didn't feel like my life, this wasn't happening to me. Then thoughts of how my wife and mum would be once Gary (my solicitor) calls them with one of the worst bits of news they are ever going to receive.

Next thing I knew I was stood in front of a counter surrounded by security officers. I placed my bags on the counter, everything was put into clear style police evidence bags, noted down, money ripped out my wallet and counted and then I was asked to take my shoes off. I can only assume they are checking them for either drugs or weapons, or to stop me from killing myself. I was patted down once more, handcuffed, which held such significance as it was the start of what was to come, this was now my life.

Being led by the wrist, like a child strapped to their parent, I was taken down the corridor to another, uncuffed, told to wear a bright stinky orange vest and pointed to go into a room which looked like a police interview room. Gary was already sat in there waiting.

He started with the most ridiculous comment, 'Well just as I thought, 5 years, straight down the line of the guidelines, how you feeling?' I felt like responding with some profanity, "How do you think I bloody feel, just been sentenced to 5 years in prison!" He then said he'd spoken to Hannah and to pass on a message that she loves me and said, don't worry about prison, time will fly! He will come and visit me in a few weeks to complete the paperwork for confiscation, then shook my hand and off he went.

I was just sat there still, in a total state of bewilderment thinking that someone will be coming soon to tell me they've made a mistake, it was either my mind going into defense mode or wishful thinking, both clearly wasn't going to change this shitty situation.

After what felt like a long wait, someone did finally come in. The same guard that led me in grabbed my wrist again and led me down yet another corridor. He shouted through me to the other guards 'What cell we sticking him in?', opened up a door and directed me in by the wrists to a room as big as a public loo cubicle.

The cell was like a dungeon in a film where you leave someone to rot and die; 3 concrete walls and a wooden style pew recessed into the back wall. I was so parched and asked in the kindest manner known to man for some water and he mumbled something before taking off the handcuffs, slamming the door behind him. I looked at my watch; it was now 4pm.

I scoured the room thinking how did people write the graffiti or gang tags or a statement like 'M&MS 4EVA' which was ironic as I wouldn't taste a M&M now for a few years.

An hour went by pretty quickly as my mind was working a million miles per hour. I didn't get my water and my mouth was like a camel's foot when finally the door opened. Time for handcuffs once more, no directions, just another game of follow the leader by dragging me by the wrist through another door out of the building and into a dark courtyard area where a SERCO van, aka The Sweat Box was waiting. He pulled me up the steps, not on purpose but because of the awkwardness of getting up the steps whilst handcuffed and told me to step into what looked like a photobooth with a plastic seat molded into the wall. The inside was bright white from the artificial lights, the windows gave the outside a pink tint and looking down the van whilst he tried to get the cuffs off with the door ajar, the van was full, like a cattle truck with other prisoners all penned in.

The door shut and I took a seat. The van was eerily quiet considering how many people were squeezed onboard as it started up and began to reverse. The gates opened and the light flooded the van. The sun beamed through the pink-tinted window as I got a glimpse of the court grounds and through the side gate I'd walked past many times on my way in.

I angled my face away from the window in case the press tried to get pictures through the windows like you see on the news, but looking back why did I even think my case was so important enough that they'd be running after the van with me inside? Cringe worthy!

I could just make out through the scratched small pinky window the places, shops and restaurants that I'd gone past on my daily journey. I looked above, and towering over, behind the buildings, was the Shard dominating the skyline. It broke my heart as it just reminded me of my wife which felt another planet away now. Memories of our wedding night in the Shard started to flood in and so did the water filling up my eyes. How it hurt, from my heart down to my stomach. It was so painful. How I wish I could just make a phone call to Hannah or a text to get her reassurance or just to tell her how much I loved her once more. That simple luxury is now over.

The driver put on the radio and Buffalo Soldier billowed through the van, which felt at the time like the anthem to the end of the world. Still wearing my court clothes which consisted of nylon trousers, when combined with the plastic seat, the driver's heavy foot and his cornering, I was flung around the bright white phone box like a rag doll. Every time he braked I'd headbutt the plastic wall in front of me, which was pretty close anyway as it was such a confined space.

When the van stopped at red lights, I felt a huge hatred feeling of jealousy seeing people going about their business. All in their summer attire, looking and staring at the van knowing that 16 prisoners were aboard on their way to prison.

Chapter 2. Prison Arrival

We arrived and I caught a glimpse of the front of the building which looked exactly as you'd expect - grim! It was a dark and scary looking old building, draped in barbed wire like an army barracks.

The big metal gates opened and the van reversed into the prison. When it came to a stop, you could sense everyone held their breath in anticipation of what was to come next like we all shared the same apprehension.

The sun was heating up the van; all I could see out the window was a wall and some of the prisoners in the van starting to get lively. It was clear that 2 of the foreign prisoners knew each other and started shouting in their native tongue which sounded pretty angry and intimidating. Unfortunately, I was stuck in between them both, one in front and one behind, as they competed to be heard.

Finally, I could feel the van rocking and people's doors started to get unlocked. As much as I tried to angle my head, I couldn't see anything and due to being last in, I was last out. The door opened, no one said anything and the guard had disappeared. I gingerly walked out, there was no one around so I walked towards the building. There was a prison officer there who said nothing apart from point sharply for me to go through the door.

Inside was a counter like you'd find at a post office, so I approached it which of course was the wrong thing to do, yet they expected me to know the process like I'd been here before. "In there with the others," barked the officer referring to the holding pen resembling a deportation centre. There weren't many English-speaking people in there and the only space I could see was at the back, typically, right next to Mr West! (My Co-Defendant)

I sat next to him and I could sense he wanted to speak to me, maybe for reassurance or the only sense of familiarity in a totally bizarre unknown territory. Prisoners were pacing, shouting, getting agitated and impatient. You could tell some of them were experienced prisoners, and like regular hotel guests wanted expedited check-in service to get to their room (prison cell) before anybody else.

Prison offers called out names one by one, which was a task in itself as the foreign speakers tried to decipher if it was theirs that had been called out as the officers made no effort to try and get the pronunciation of the names right.

All people spoke about in the holding pen was how long did each other get as a sentence and what did they end up in prison for; this seemed to be the universal prison language.

Weirdly, but thankfully, not one person asked me and they seemed to give me a wide birth. I'd later find out from speaking to one of the guys who was in there with me that everyone thought I was an officer or solicitor as I sat in my white shirt, trousers and shoes while everyone else seemed to be wearing tracksuits.

Finally, my turn and 'HOCKEY' got shouted out. I was summoned over to the counter, wondering why they couldn't do this the first time round. Fingerprints taken, which again seemed to annoy the officer as I took my finger off too early, something which happened twice before he barked "KEEP YOUR FINGER ON THERE UNTIL I TELL YOU TO REMOVE IT". It would have helped if he'd given me that direction before we started.

Next, I was told to stand back onto a black mat on the floor which had 2 painted footprints on it. Again, I managed to get on his bad side as I was telepathically meant to know he wanted me to stare down a camera lens behind his head. I was dismissed promptly back to the pigpen.

I spotted a water dispenser on my way back; I wasn't even going to ask and grabbed a plastic cup that rested on top as quickly as I could and filled it and chucked it down my neck before sitting back down next to Jay. It was probably the best water I'd ever tasted as I was that desperate.

West, keeping a keen eye on me, used this opportunity as an ice- breaker. He asked where I got the water from and then what did I just have to do before making my way back into the holding pen. Then he turned the conversation to our case, stating "It isn't over" in an overly optimistic voice and that he will fight it and appeal it. There was so much I wanted to say so him. West had not spoken to me in years, and instead of trying to defend the case, Jay stood in court and blamed everything falsely on me. West was the cause of so many of the charges I ended up being convicted of, as we were co-charged, while the majority of my own charges were Not Guilty as I stood and gave evidence and my defense to the Jury. The visions of causing him physical harm rather than having a pleasant conversation was the only thing at the forefront of my mind but I'm not a fighter. To be honest, it was ok to have a slice of normality and a brief conversation in this awfully frightening and intimidating place was welcome.

He got called shortly after and I was called by a different officer this time where I was directed into another room. It was full of large black shoe boxes from floor to ceiling, there was a scanning machine like you'd find at an airport and a counter at the back. To the left, was a weirdly placed shower curtain and my bag that I had not seen since court.

I was told due to the size of the bag and number of contents that they wouldn't be able to process it today and I'd need to wait until tomorrow. "Behind the shower curtain, fella" some fat, short officer said as he came in. "Shirt off". This was the dreaded strip search. I knew what was coming. Trousers were next, followed by socks, then boxers. How degrading!

Now, standing in my birthday suit, meat and two veg on parade and if that wasn't bad enough, I was asked to do a slow spin. I was half expecting fingers up the bum but luckily that never happened. After I'd spun round like a slow cooked chicken, the officer joked that it was just his job and glad we got it over and done with and I can put my clothes back on. How kind.

I was just about to put my own clothes back on when another officer pulled the curtain open and chucked in some grey rags and grabbed my clothes as he said, "Put them on mate, that's all we got". It was a pair of oversized grey prison issue tracksuit bottoms and a large burgundy t-shirt wrapped inside. I'd binned clothes in better condition. They stank of sweat and everything was as holey as a church. At least it semi-fit, as I'd seen people walking around in the prison gear looking like they had a crop top on or a potato sack with how ill-fitting their issued clothing was.

To top it off, he said there were no more prison issue shoes left, so here are your court shoes. What a numpty I looked with grey joggers, burgundy t-shirt and black court shoes on. If I'd had a red nose I could probably charge to do children's parties as Bobo the prison clown. I thanked them for their time and as I walked out, I think pity took over an officer due to my kind gesture which was probably out the ordinary for them, and one of them chased after me with a brand-new pair of Velcro shoes still in their cellophane. There is a God after all!

The same guy walked me out and pointed to a small hatch in the wall down the corridor. Curry, rice and what looked like nuggets were being served to all new arrivals by another prisoner. I don't like curry, so I chose nuggets and rice. I was shooed into another pen next door, but no one was in it this time which was nice. I was so hungry, I delved into the food. The rice was dry and like bullets but at least I had the nuggets to fill me up. I took one bite into one and spat it out; I'd been conned. They were vegetarian nuggets!

A few minutes later, yet another officer appeared to escort me upstairs and put me into another packed holding room. A gangster looking black guy with his hands down his pants addresses me; "Hey B, what you in here for ?" I just answered short and sharply, "Fraud" without elaborating further. "B, we all thought you were a pig or a legal bod downstairs cuz". As he wanted to engage in conversation with me, I asked the same question in return. "Knife point robbery, allegedly". I asked no further questions and he carried on lacing his shoes like it was the first time that he'd done so.

One by one, prisoners left and didn't return until it was my turn. I was led into a makeshift doctor's office with a nurse sat at the computer. She asked me to sit down and was began to ask a series of questions. Every question was orientated around either drugs, drink, mental health, substance abuse, self-harming or suicide.

I sat there and answered confidently and convincingly "No" to each one of her questions. She looked at me as though I was an imposter. She turned to me in a confused manner and said, "Sorry, I don't normally ask, but if it's not drug or drink related, what are you in here for?" I'm asking myself the same question, I thought. "Fraud", I answered. I think this definitely wouldn't the last time I'd be answering those questions. She said, "Well done you for keeping healthy" and then asked how I'm feeling now I'm in prison and was I expecting it. I'd read that they mentally assess you when you come into prison to see where you fit for categorization and also suicide watch.

I told her I'd been on bail for 3 and a half years and was convicted a week ago. Apart from the initial shock of finally landing here in HMP's finest, I knew it was coming and I was ok. I think I passed with flying colours and she was sympathetic, talking about if I changed my mind about how I felt how to come back for help.

Next, I was waved across the hall to a little office with an officer who had my photo that had been taken downstairs. There were so many of them printed on an A4 page which he could peel off like stickers to put on different folders and files that had my name on them. He passed me my ID card, but when I looked down I saw it said "HACKY". I was quick to point out the error, which he didn't take too kindly to. "Well, it is your face and date of birth isn't it?".

I just nodded, to which he replied, "Well, we all make mistakes and it doesn't affect you does it ? So, smoker's pack or nonsmoker's pack ?".

Well, "I don't smoke", I said and also "I need to call my wife". He just handed me a small slip with codes on it. I asked how I used that to make a call to which he replied, "Ask an officer on your wing". As helpful as ever!

"Go see the workers on the middle of the desk in the hallway and get your nonsmoker's pack and bedding". 2 prisoners were stood behind an island in the middle of the hallway. They dumped a clear bin bag which was full of the cheapest of cheap produce you could think of; all unbranded, long-life milk, chocolate, tea bags, sugar, some coffee sachets. Plonked alongside it was some dog bedding. It was a bobbly old orange blanket, something your nan would have knitted back in the war. A green sheet that had seen better days and riddled with pubes, and a pillowcase that I'm sure had been used to mop the floor.

Gone are the days of memory foam, Egyptian cotton and duck feather duvets. Yet another guard, more stairs the other side of the hallway, back down and through another set of doors.

I'm now on the prison wing. It was 8:30pm, with no prisoners around which I was thankful for, but this was it, I'M IN PRISON! I'd seen this scene so many times on prison programmes or films and it was literally like stepping into a film set. Never did I think I'd be in this situation, EVER. My mouth was dry, palms sweaty and I felt ever so small. This was an intimidating place that's for sure, not that I let it show on the outside.

So many thoughts were going through my head. How the hell did I end up here, how the hell am I going to get through this extremely long sentence and who the hell is going to be my cell mate?

Knowing its late and I'm just about to be banged up with a total stranger, a bloody prisoner, that thought alone took over me. What if he doesn't speak a word of English, what if we don't get on at all and what if he was a total nutcase!

Another prisoner appeared out of nowhere. He filled in a card with my details for his reference and said, "You're on floor 3 mate, up the stairs behind you, the officer will let you in your cell".

I could physically feel my heart pounding out my neck as I gathered my worldly goods. Yes, the bag of shit and dog bedding, and made my way upstairs to the 3rd floor of E Wing in Wandsworth prison.

Looking around, it was a blue and cream themed wing; the walls were cream and the doors and banisters and rails were blue. It was eerily quiet. I could see another officer in the distance as the other had stopped on another floor. I made my way towards him and could hear the stereotypical jingling of keys resonating around the empty landing as he walked towards door 304. "This is you mate" as he unlocked the cell door. Inside I was trembling as I squeezed by him and through the door to get inside the cell.

Inside there he was, my cell mate, medium build, on his hands and knees scrubbing the floor, shirtless, the cell reeked of chemical products. He stood up. I didn't know the prison etiquette so I just stuck out my hand and said, "Hi I'm Daniel." Luckily he returned the gesture. "Bobby", he replied and shook my hand. With that the door slammed behind us.

I felt relieved that the initial dreaded moment was over. I had a quick scour round the room. Bunk beds on my left, a desk affixed to the wall on my right, with 2 chairs, a cupboard above that and immediately to my right, next to the door, was a small TV and miniature kettle. Towards the end of the bunks was a sink in the wall like you'd find at a public loo and a toilet covered by a shower curtain.

Still clinging onto my things, Bobby took the lead. "This is you man" and pointed to a cupboard on the other side of the desk, he pulled out a cardboard box from under the bunk. "You're welcome to use this too for your things, Here let me help you make your bed". Just these few kind gestures made me feel instantly relaxed.

Bobby also seemed relieved at my arrival, and in a strong cockney accent said, "Man, I'm so glad they put someone normal in here with me, bruv. They sorted me out today, done me a right favour". It turned out he had a string of previous cell mates that he didn't get on with, including a guy that wrote all over the cell walls whilst still asleep. Another peed all over the floor, and finally there had been a serial killer.

Conversation soon turned to what we were both in for, and he went first. He would steal high-end goods such as Canada Goose jackets and other designer clothing, but obviously his luck ran out. He only had a week to go on his 6-week sentence. I was pleased for him to be getting out so soon but even more disappointed for myself. Just getting comfortable with my first cell mate and already he'll soon be going and I'd get another new cell mate.

I was so jealous that he only had a week while I had 2 and a half years. He offered me a cup of tea as I started to talk about my ordeal over the past 2 months in court. He was fascinated as I told him about the service I provided for clients, the amounts involved, how it got investigated and how it played out in court. "You were stitched there, bruv. Man I feel for you, bro". I think I chewed his ear off for the next hour about how wronged I felt and the shock of now ending up in prison.

Conversation then turned to family on the outside. He had 2 kids that thought he was currently in hospital and I told him about how much I missed my wife and Tess. Bless him, he was so supportive and showed empathy and related to my heartbreak having himself been in and out of prisons since he was 15; he's now 33.

He looked slightly familiar and the more I looked at him, the more he resembled Plan B, the rapper, crossed with Mike Skinner from The Streets. I felt like I needed to sponge as much information from this prison veteran as I could before he left in a week's time. How to get by, how to act, how to hold yourself. I was so grateful that he could see I was like a deer in the headlights and reassured me that it's nothing like the horror stories you hear.

"Listen, nothing bad's going to happen to you in here, bro, I promise you that." It was so comforting for him to be so caring and trying to put my mind at rest, clearly seeing the nerves and pain in my eyes and voice. "Man, you're not from round here so you have no problem with the gangs. You're clearly a sound guy and just keep your head down and do your time, you'll have no problems, bro".

The proof would be in the pudding when the doors open at 8am in the morning. I asked Bobby how to make a call as I was desperate to call Hannah, but the cell had no phone as it had been nicked. I also had no cups, plates, cutlery or pillow. Again, Bobby said he would take me under his wing and related how he felt the first time in prison all those years ago. He made a list of all my missing items and said he would go on a treasure hunt in the morning.

I'll always be thankful to Bobby for being so comforting and reassuring, and considering where I was, it could have been a lot worse. He made me feel more prepared and confident to take on the second day inside jail.

Finishing our conversation around midnight, Bobby crawled into the bottom bunk. I took the hint that he was probably tired and also bored of my rambling on by now, so I went for my first official pee in jail. This felt awkward in itself, like Bobby was watching and listening to every last little drip.

Stage fright took over and it felt like an eternity to finish the stream. This is definitely something I'm going to have to get used to. Up I climbed to the top bunk by leaping off one of the chairs from the desk. Lying on my makeshift pillow which was stuffed with clothing, I pulled up the orange stinky itchy blanket and stared at the flaky cracked ceiling.

I felt myself welling up once again as I started to think about my wife lying in our bed with an empty space beside her where I would normally be. Tess in the next room wondering where her dad would be, with no normal bedtime routine, no bedtime story from daddy and with mummy brushing her teeth instead of daddy. No bedtime kiss, and I won't be there in the morning when she wakes.

I wanted to crawl up and bawl like a baby, but I kept swallowing it and just wanted the worst day of my life to be over. I'm no longer Daniel the husband, Dad or Son. I'm now prisoner A29*** of Wandsworth Prison. The bed was so uncomfortable, it was like a pilates mat on top of a park bench. As I closed my eyes, I wanted to go from a living nightmare to a dream just to take a break from this unbelievable day.

I finally nodded off, only to be woken an hour later with someone kicking their cell door in. It frightened the life out of me as I sat up startled. The screams that accompanied it were like a sound effect you'd use on Halloween; blood curdling, like someone was being murdered. The sound of quick footsteps followed by the noise of jangling keys going past our cell door. My heart was pounding but the only reassurance I could give myself was that the cell door was firmly locked and no-one was getting in.

Eventually I got back to sleep and woke up every hour until 7am, when I couldn't hold it in any longer and jumped down for a wee. I didn't get it all out the night before as I was bursting. The sound of gushing water woke Bobby and he gave me a kind "Morning Mate" as I washed my hands.

I apologised if I woke him, to which he replied that I hadn't, but I think he was just being polite. He asked me how I'd slept and how I was feeling to which, I said "OK, considering", but it was an awful night's sleep. There was a nano second when I woke this morning that I thought, when I opened my eyes, I was back home in my bed and half expected to see my wife. Reality hit me like a punch to the stomach when I realised I was still in a dream state and this nightmare is my reality.

8:30am came and you could hear the commotion getting louder and louder as everyone was waiting to get out to the traps. I stood staring out the gateway to Hell through the little window cut into the door.

I had the feeling that I would stand out like a sore thumb in this place and would be a prime target. I heard keys jangling and the door was opened. The quiet wing that I'd entered last night was now filled with testosterone, blokes of all ethnicities, no one talked, everyone just shouted to each other like they were on a football terrace.

I took a few steps out of the cell and held on to the railing to observe and face head-on my first full day of prison life. Do I put on a hard man face like, don't mess with me, or do I just keep neutral, play it by ear and say a polite "Morning" to anyone who made eye contact. I decided to do the latter.

There were people going out of one cell into another, people with toiletries and towels over their shoulders hastily making their way towards the showers, people shouting from floor to floor. Bobby shot out, true to his word, to get my things from the list he made last night.

I made my way to the ground floor where an officer stood in the middle of all the commotion. I asked where the applications were to request a prison transfer nearer to the South Coast and an application to have my telephone numbers approved to my phone pin. The officer, who was surrounded by foreign speakers trying to get across in their best English what it was that they needed, finally answered me. "It could take months, mate. You also need to be categorised first", as he handed me a form to complete. I was deflated and needed to get advice from Bobby when I got back to the cell.

People passed me going about their business as I made my way back up the stairs. I tried my "Morning" method to people who made eye contact, and to my surprise some even responded with "Alright mate." Others didn't, but you can't win them all.

The stereotype and pre-judgement I had on prisoners quickly subsided as I made my way back to the cell unscathed. Bobby wasn't back yet and I sat at the desk and started to fill out the forms. I didn't see the next blow coming as Bobby, clutching a stash of goods for me including a cell phone, said, "I'm moving !". I froze, went numb, was devastated, crushed and under a false sense of security being under Bobby's wing since arriving.

In an instant, thoughts and apprehensions came flooding back as I knew a new cellmate would be imminent. The same thoughts overcame me; Who will I get next, what will they be like, what if we don't get on, why did Bobby want to leave?

Bobby was friends with the guy across the landing, his cell mate had moved block today and his cell space is vacant so he'd asked Bobby to move in.

He kept reassuring me I'll be ok as he quickly packed all his belongings into the box and told me he'll look out for me from across the landing. I had to keep telling myself I've known this guy

less than a day and need to get used to this, and will experience it multiple times before my sentence is up. I had to get a grip as in a blink of an eye he was gone.

I knew I had moments before they plonked someone else in Bobby's space, so I grabbed my bedding from the top bunk and in a flash

moved into the prime real estate, the bottom bunk. No more climbing up for me!

CHAPTER 3. THE BODY ODOR WAS OVERWHELMING

The cell door opened and it only happened to be the guy I was sat with in the holding cell who thought I was a solicitor. My heart dropped.

When I say I could smell him before I saw him it's an understatement; he honked! He didn't recognise me or recall our conversation from yesterday. "Yo, B, which one's me?" I pointed to the top bunk. He just nodded and said, "I'm T".

T was a skinny, 38-year-old black male with a strong accent so I found it hard to understand what he was saying and kept asking him to repeat what he had said. Politely, seeing him clinging on to his very few, belongings, I said he could use the cupboard that Bobby had just vacated.

I gave him some space to sort himself out, make his bed etc. and started to finish the forms. I found concentrating difficult as I kept getting constant wafts of body odour which was overwhelming. After he made his bed, he turned hunter gatherer, looking at anything Bobby had left in the cupboard or around the cell. He found a used roll-on which he cleaned under the tap and immediately used, to my relief. However, it just masked, temporarily, the pong that filled the room.

He was reading documents that Bobby had left, going through bags of rubbish and eating prison issue biscoffee biscuits Bobby had left lying around.

Under the bed was discarded clothing Bobby had hoarded. T held them up one by one, giving them scrutiny as to which ones he would keep for himself. I found him sketchy compared to Bobby and slightly uncomfortable like I had to watch myself and what I said around him.

Finally I finished the app, so back to the officer downstairs I went before they locked us away, leaving T in the cell to get comfortable. On my return I bumped into Bobby at the top of the landing. "Come showers, bro, before they bang you up" I think he was again taking me under his wing, knowing that was another one of my concerns, and specifically all the horror stories about prisons and showers!

I took him up on the offer, ran back into my cell to get my towels and shower gel sachets. Bobby was not fazed about prison showers, and laughed at my fears of being bummed in the shower or stabbed up. Walking in, the floor was littered with sachets or used shampoo and gel, and the room looked like a shower from a public swimming pool back in the year 1750!

To my surprise, everyone showering wasn't naked. Due to being an induction wing, most people on E block were new arrivals too and regardless of the hard exterior, must have shared the same reservations as everyone stood showering in boxers.

One became free, I got in and got on with it, giving the boxers a good rinse at the same time as everybody else did. The general conversations going on was about how bad in was in this hell hole compared to other prisons they had been in. Like hearing a real-life TripAdvisor for prisons! Food is better in that prison, accommodation is better in this prison and if you get to this said prison, you get a duvet on arrival.

10 mins later I was done, jumped back into the prison clobber and was back in the cell just in time for them to lock the door behind me. The first experience out in the wild was over. I was still intact.

A sense of relief came over me. The perception I had of prison and inmates was poles apart from what I had just witnessed. Although, there was still an underlying current that things could go sour pretty quickly, so I wouldn't be dropping my guard any time soon.

The cell was now thick with the scent of T. He was on the phone and I just caught the end of the conversation with him saying, "Don't worry about the guns, G." Alarm bells started ringing that this guy had not been telling me the truth yesterday about his alleged knife crime.

Seeing me come back in the room, he finished his call pretty sharpish, took the piece of paper he was holding and flushed it down the toilet. As I hung up my wet items, he began to make conversation. "Yo, B, how long you been here for ?" I thought he was taking the piss as we'd arrived together and had the same conversation yesterday. It was now my turn to put him to the test and see if he would give me the same answer as yesterday when I ask him, again, what he is in for. "Case of mistaken identity," he replied. Apparently a robbery at a shop at knifepoint and he just happened to be in the wrong place at the wrong time. "Well, they said they caught a man at the scene that was described to them, that looked like me, but I was holding no samurai sword and lock knife in my pocket".

He was caught red handed at the scene, so how is it allegedly mistaken identity? I kept trying to tell myself who am I to question the truth, but then again, not knowing who I'm sharing a cell with does make me feel uneasy.

He was awaiting a trial which would start in a month's time, but felt there was enough to discredit their case and he was certain he would get off. Next the conversation turned to religion, not by my choice. I was quick to add I'm not religious and he was flummoxed.

"You got to believe in something, B" and proceeded to tell me how he had been a Christian, then Muslim and now he's a spiritualist. He believes in nature, loves birds and believes in aliens.

It's ironic how someone so spiritual, bird loving, nature loving yet samurai sword wielding shop robber is preaching to me about religion. Time did fly though and by the time we finished our chat, it was lunch time and the door was unlocked once more.

The guard shouted "FOOD"! and across the landing to the right you could see a glow coming out of an open door from the hot plates. Inside were 3 prisoners serving slop from metal kitchen trolleys.

The choice today was a pie, fish, rice, gammon with a side order of potatoes. You get to choose 2 items. I went for gammon and rice thinking cleverly that the rice would keep me fuller for longer. The last worker at the end delved into a box, "Banana or Cake". I chose the cake and he handed me a frozen chocolate ring doughnut and a sandwich bag containing tea bags, porridge, sachets of sugar and milk whiteners.

Lastly, he handed me a carton of UHT milk made for a child and making my way out, was a table just outside the door with mountains of loafs of bread. "White or Brown ?" said another prisoner, handing over 4 slices of bread to go with the meal and 4 little pots of butter.

The gammon was that fatty if I got served it at any other place than here, I'd have sent it back. T finally made his way back to the cell and the guard locked the door behind us. The rice was freezing and flavourless, the gammon was enough for a mouthful, so I eventually resorted to making a sandwich with it all to at least provide me with a substantial meal.

Thoughts turned to simple things like ketchup and salt and pepper. Things that you take for granted but in here are luxury. T scoffed everything but the plate, and seeing I was nearly finished hacking around the fat, his attention turned to my plate. Well, if I wasn't going to have it, he may as well but it was like having a dog staring at you as you finished eating.

The cell door opened again and the officer flung in a bag which contained my belongings from yesterday. It was such a nice surprise like getting a slice of home brought to the door.

Fresh boxers, socks, writing pads, pens, pencils, books, earbuds, 2 pictures, facewipes, towel from home, flipflops... I sniffed each item to get a scent of home and quickly put the items away before someone else laid claim to them.

I just sat on my bed clinging to the 2 pictures my wife had packed. Both were of the HOCKEY tribe; Me, Tess and

Hannah. It tugged on my heart strings so much. I just stared and stared at them, felt sorry for myself and felt sorry for them. How I missed them so much, the pain was like a sharp stabbing pain straight to the heart.

It was Saturday so I wondered what Tess and Hannah would be up to as normally we went for family day out at the weekend. Then I remembered Bobby got me the phone this morning and that scrappy bit of paper handed to me yesterday. Even though my numbers aren't on yet, if T was able to make a call this must be the emergency reception call that everyone gets.

I could finally speak to my wife for the first time since prison, and I followed the instructions printed on the slip followed by my personal pin. I felt nervous, anxious and excited all at the same time. It rang and she answered in a shocked and surprised state. "Hello, babe, it's me." She cried whilst screaming 'baby' down the phone.

It was so warming and reassuring just to hear her voice. I asked, "Are you ok?" She said, "Not really, I've cried since you got sentenced and I'm at your sisters at the moment with your Mum. They're all here." I shouted "Hello" to everyone before trying to reassure

Hannah of my safety and gave first impressions of what prison life was life. "I'm fine in here, babe, please don't worry about me. I don't feel unsafe, there's guards everywhere and I've already used the showers but I'm missing you guys so so much. I love you".

Hannah then went on to ask for reassurance that I'll still want her after all of this. "Of course, you and Tess are all that's keeping me going and gives me something to work towards. We are married, silly, I love you with all my heart, nothing changes that, just feels like I'm frozen in time here!" It was just what she wanted to hear. The phone started to bleep so I said I think my credit was going to go. We got our final "Loves you's" in a million times over before I heard my Mum's voice shout, "We all love you and are thinking of you and should be able to come visit Wednesday". With that, the phone cut off.

I'd definitely put on a braver persona than I really felt as I didn't want them worrying about me on the outside on top of everything else, and I'm sure I did enough to convince them.

I sat back down on my bed looking at their pictures once more. I was distraught and never felt so alone. I was inconsolable on the inside but on the outside, with T now sat on the bunk above me, I remained strong as much as I wanted to break down.

Sensing the silence, T shouted "Yo B, you alright?" I said I'd just spoken to the wife and my mother which I found more difficult than I thought. He peered over from above and when he saw I was clinging onto the pictures, he jumped down. "You mind if I take a look, B?" I handed him the pictures. "Man, you been blessed, B. I can't imagine what it feels like as I have no family on the outside".

He explained that he only had bredrin's, friends that look out for him that he classes as his family. I asked if he was part of any gangs, which he said he used to be when younger but not anymore.

It looks as though T wasn't aware he was coming to prison as he had absolutely nothing with him, unlike me who packed everything in preparation. He asked what else I brought into the prison and I listed everything I've had given to me so far, including 2 books I brought into read. His face lit up and he asked if he could read one.

As a bonding gesture I obliged and handed him one to read. He went back up pleased with his new possession and started to read. I put my pictures next to me and started to write a letter to Hannah. My pen bled tears on the page. I wrote my whole experience from court to first night in prison and pledged how much I loved and missed her.

I had to stop writing every paragraph to muster up the courage to keep writing as it was emotionally draining, and also my hand ached from not writing a letter in so long.

Writing my wife's name and address on the envelope was also a struggle. Since coming to prison I'd definitely gone soppy and to mush with my emotions which I'd never had an issue with before. It was just a stark reminder of the separation and distance between us, with her being back at home in the south and me stuck in a prison in London. Next mission when the door is unlocked is to hunt down the post box.

Whilst writing the letter, I decided to write this book and share my observations, feelings and life before and during prison as this situation I find myself in, luckily, most won't ever get to experience or go through in their lives.

At 5pm, there was some commotion outside the door and it was unlocked. 2 guards were at the door and a worker with 3 pallets on a roller stopped at our threshold. It was food.

CHAPTER 4. SAUSAGE ROLL AND SUBLIMINAL MESSAGES

At the weekends, you get a hot meal for lunch and cold food for dinner. During the week you get a cold lunch at 11:30 and hot meal around 4:30-5. The choice for this evening was a sausage roll, cheese and tuna baguette or vegetable pasty. I was given the sausage roll and handed a pack of 2 biscoffee biscuits and a bag of cheese and onion Seabrook crisps.

As sorry as the sausage roll looked and how I hated them cold previously, this was a sight for sore eyes and I demolished the lot. 6pm rolled on, on TV The Simpsons came on which brought back memories of sitting with Tess watching and laughing at the programme together.

T was a fan of the Simpsons, too, and we both sat on my bed at the bottom of the bunk and killed another half an hour eating sausage rolls, watching Simpsons. Outside the cell was a wash of noise from people shouting to each other through the gap in the door frames where the hinges were, keys jangling, people banging their doors constantly and footsteps from officers patrolling the landings.

It made me feel apprehensive like someone was always going to come in or I was going to be moved any minute. The environment is going to take some getting used to. We passed the time just by watching crap on TV, a universal choice was Grand Designs, Police Interceptors and a programme about Harry and Megan Markle's wedding.

T would often make comments about everything having a double or secret meaning, everything had a subliminal message which he was receiving. In the adverts he would provide me with his theories and how the government are trying to dumb down children as they are getting smarter, all of which made me feel extremely uncomfortable. I let him have his say and gave no response.

The worst was when we started to watch a film at 9pm on Film 4, Mission Impossible. It was impossible for us to watch without him receiving some kind of message that only he could see. I'd already seen this one previously but figured it would kill another 2 hours, then it would be time for bed, another day done.

As soon as the film started, so did T, asking me questions whether I'd seen this before and do I remember this version. I informed him I had seen it but it was a little while ago, but I don't recall the start. "I KNEW IT" and started uncontrollably laughing, but there wasn't anything funny on the TV, it was all action at the beginning of the film. I felt freaked out and sat there in silence, intently starting at the tv. "Sorry, B, I won't talk through it, I can see I'm annoying you". I think he realised his behavior was coming across as peculiar and I wasn't on the same wavelength as him.

It was the weirdest experience ever sat watching a film with someone analysing every scene, and despite his pledge at the beginning the comments throughout kept rolling in. Once it was finished, I crawled into my pit while he said he was going to stay up and watch tv, and did I mind if he left the tv on ? Well, what choice did I have, I didn't want to get stabbed up! Unfortunately, sharing a cell also means that you need to take into account their routine, habits, annoyances and, of course, smells!

The combination of the smell, tv in the background and metal bunk bed shaking every time he turned to get comfy or jumping up and down to use the loo or sink kept me lying awake thinking of my family. I eventually cried myself to sleep, it was all too much.

I woke around 3am to what sounded like a fire alarm going off, followed by a lot of jingling keys and fast footsteps. The sound must be an emergency alarm for the guards who were running to the location to help with whatever pandemonium was going on. Another night full of broken sleep, door drumming from the neighbours and someone who thought it would be a great idea to keep singing through the crack of his door. Seems it woke T too as he was boiling the kettle and asked if I wanted a cuppa.

I don't really like hot drinks so declined gracefully but it didn't stop him asking for tea bags, milk and sugar. Why don't I just drink it for him too, for the full set! I happily donated the items from the bag of crap I got when I was processed at Reception. The scavenger's eyes lit up!

I stayed in bed until 7:30am, with the news on the TV (a nice universal programme to agree on), then I dragged myself out of bed, got dressed in my greys, brushed teeth, made the bed, trainers on, which felt amazing as they were finally my own trainers from the bag I received yesterday, and I waited anxiously for my second day running the gauntlet.

The door opened at 8:30am and the big chunky door clunked open, "S&D's" the guard shouted in as he pushed the door open. I take it that's social and domestic, time to get everything done before they lock you up again.

Feeling a little more confident than yesterday, I picked up the letter I wrote to the wife and went on a mission to find the post box. As soon as I stepped onto the landing the siren sounded again, the same noise that woke me at 3am.

I looked over the railings below to see 10 guards run to the right to a cell, a minute later emerging and shouting "Get Back" as they carried him like a horizontal plank of wood through the crowd that had gathered to watch the action unfold.

Watching on, I spotted a red box bolted on the wall across the landing to the right, and I walked over passing some mean looking individuals, the type that looked like they'd shank you just for looking in their direction, but I passed without any issue. The A4 water marked, food covered page on the front of the box read 'POST BOX, 8:30 COLLECTION'. That's today's post missed then!

I wish the post was instant as she won't receive that letter now for days. I looked over the railings again, this time from the other side of the landing, and could see a door open which seemed to lead outside, another experience I needed to get over and done with.

The horror stories that you hear and watch on TV and movies. The 'Yard' is where muscle heads hang out, hustles are done, drug deals, scores are settled and gangs are formed, all out of sight of the guards. If I got 2 and a half years, I need to get over this fear as I was in desperate need just for some fresh air, air that didn't stink of body odour.

I walked across the landing, down the steps and past many cells that were billowing out a variety of smells from strong alcohol, cleaning products, smoke, weed and sweat. I finally made it to the door which led to outside. There was a guard on the door and he looked like he wished he was anywhere else in the world but yard duty. Down some metal steps, and there I was, feeling like a lamb to the slaughter in a real-life prison yard.

I felt like Andy from Shawshank Redemption as other prisoners circled, anticlockwise, the small area penned in by metal fences topped with barbed wire. Before sticking out like a deer in the headlights, I started walking. The fear soon faded when I was overwhelmed with how great it felt to be outside in the open with the sun hitting my face and fresh air in my lungs.

In the corner of the year was 4 pieces of outside gym equipment which were all occupied by people working out. The stereotypical big blokes who liked to pump iron and full of steroids it was not. It was just normal looking men working out.

Looking around whilst doing my anti clockwise laps there was young men who didn't look old enough to be in prison, old men who looked like someone's grandad and totally out of place, and other normal looking people in their own clothes who looked like they were just visiting for the day.

Don't get me wrong, there were also some nasty looking fuckers, people who you wouldn't want to get on the wrong side of. This Polish guy, a massive man mountain, just shadow boxing right in the middle of the yard, like an exhibition, everyone just let him get on with it and went about their own business.

I thought I'd walk right into a war zone stepping outside but my perception was incorrect to my relief. As time went on prisoners had brought their towels out and were lying in the sun soaking up the rays, each ethnicity seemed to huddle in their own groups having a chin wag and now there seemed to be 2 guards at the door which filled me with more confidence.

I spotted Bobby and his new cell mate coming into the yard which was a sight for sore eyes. "How's smelly bollox ?" was his cell mate, Brett's, greeting which broke the ice. I laughed, probably over-enthusiastically trying to make a new prison ally.

I said, "Stinky, but he's alright, just a bit strange". I could have worse, that's for sure, as weird as that sounds as he was very peculiar. Bobby was happy to see me, introduced us officially and asked if I was alright and how was I getting on. It was nice to know someone cared.

We did a few more laps and I joined in their conversations trying to win brownie points before getting back to the cell to try and squeeze in a shower before we get banged up again. T was sat on the top bunk reading the book again. "You not going out today, its lovely out there ?". He said he was happy in the cell. "I'm off to take a shower, mate, you coming ?", thinking maybe he feared going into the shower block alone. "No point, B, I only got these clothes. No point getting clean to get changed back into dirty clothes." I think he's missed the point of showering altogether. I did feel sorry for him, though, and the smell was engulfing the cell and visitors had stopped coming to the cell due to the stench. "T, I've got a spare brand-new pair of boxers and socks which you are more than welcome to, least you got something clean to change into", hoping that would overcome his reasons for not showering as well as helping him out. He was thankful and took them gladly, but my attempts failed. He still didn't shower.

It was bliss; I got a hot shower today which was rare. I washed the boxers that I had on at the same time and looked forward to changing into fresh ones that I'd brought in with me and will hang up the wet ones in the cell to dry which seemed the thing to do. That's shower no. 2 ticked off without any issues. It must have been good timing as by the time I hung my towel and boxers out to dry the guards came to lock the door.

With the TV blaring in the background as T watched re-runs of sitcoms such as the Big Bang Theory, I started writing to my mum. I penned the experience of the past 24 hours, court, sentencing and prison and how much I missed her. As I rummaged in my drawer of stationary bits for an envelope to send it, the door opened. "Induction!" Across the wing was a room next to where we get the food.

CHAPTER 5. INDUCTION

Inside the induction room was a classroom style layout. A few desks in the middle and computers lining the outside of the room. A worker (prisoner) explained the days you could kit change, swapping dirty laundry and bedding for clean ones, how to order canteen which was like a tuck shop for prisoners and everything else you need to request needs to be put on general application forms.

The computers were used to test everyone's basic learning skills with standardised Maths and English tests. I got a Level 1 for Maths, which was top, and Level 2 for English, which is average, which surprised me! I'm sure it was wrong! Once complete, the scores were written on a card by the worker and a list of 5 or so prison jobs were offered which consisted of chef, cleaner, painter, classes of education or a radio production course.

I selected the radio production course and was told it may take about 13 WEEKS to get me on the course as I handed back my form and was ushered quickly by the guard waiting outside the room to take me back to the cell.

What a waste of time that was, but I guess it's just what I needed, to waste more time and be out my cell. It took T a while longer to complete the test than me which was nice to have the room to myself as I watched crap daytime TV for the next hour until he returned, it was like heaven!

Door flings open, in walks 'smelly bollox' who jumps up to his pit and continued to read his book and I carried on with my letters to mum, Tess and wife. I took the time to write more of this book till my hand ached and when I looked at the time it was almost time for lunch. I peered out of our peep hole in the door and could see the glow from the kitchen door. Not long after the doors opened, same process yet again; however, with it being Sunday, chicken leg and spuds. Back to the cell, I inhaled the chicken, I was so hungry and the chicken was so so good. I scraped the plate, washed the plate, sat on my bed and carried on with my book. I thought the time flew and I must have been writing for ages because the next time I looked up to check it was 5pm!

6pm, which meant Simpsons on Channel 4. I could already see a pattern forming to the days, the evening was pretty much a replica of the night before, just a different film.

Monday morning, I woke up at 6am from the doors being slammed from people being taken to court for their trials, appearances or sentencing. I did the same routine as the 2 previous mornings until 8am. "2nd day screening" the guard shouted as he unlocked the door.

"2nd day? How odd", I thought, since I've been here since Friday. They called it that as during the week, the 2nd day you would have another health check, but they don't operate over the weekend.

I was pointed to the far left of the landing to wait at the locked gates. The guard from the other side opened up and led us down some stairs and into what looked like a dated hospital waiting room. Looks like me and T were first in. It was a complete shambles as the nurse came into the room and shouted "Next" and about 3 people all stood up at same time, and whoever got to her first was seen. I didn't see the point in rushing, I was of out the cell and it wasn't like I was going anywhere else.

Looking around, it was such a mix of ethnicities which seemed to be the only people talking in their native tongue. Polish and Arabic accents filled the room with sound, they were also the ones that seemed to pace a lot.

It was now at the stage that most had been seen and the nurse started shouting 'Who haven't I seen ?". I guess it was only me left. She measured my height, weight and then asked for a piss sample. They were checking people for STDs, apparently. After going to use the loo, with NO lock, trying to concentrate with all the commotion in the waiting room, it didn't help with people keep walking in over and over not knowing it occupied and no lock on the door. The task was made even worse with trying to aim into the smallest test tube which I eventually catched enough drips to fill the tube.

Handing it back to the nurse all warm and yellow was pretty embarrassing. 'HOCKEY' I was called by yet another nurse into a makeshift doctor's office. She took my blood pressure then asked me a list of multiple questions all relating to drugs and drink dependency. Like the first nurse I saw when I arrived, she too was shocked when I answered "No" to all her questions. She said the final test was a blood test. I hated blood tests and they always nearly make me pass out. I was so relieved when she said it's just a pin prick in the finger.

What didn't help was she had to squeeze my finger as hard as possible for a prolonged period of time for any blood to finally come out. I felt the room darkening and was overpowered by an overwhelming sweaty sickness feeling. She just stopped before I was going to call a halt to it myself!

She could see the state I was in and laughed before telling me to take a seat. A male nurse was waiting at the door, after she finished typing up her notes on the computer, and I was asked to go with him for an x-ray.

I was led down some more steps and stairs into a room, in the bowels of this grotty prison, where there was a state-of-the-art chest X-ray machine. I think it was being used to detect some type of respiratory disease. After that, back up to the waiting room where a guard led me back to the cell.

It was now around 11:30. I couldn't believe how long that all took; it was brilliant, another morning ticked off! The trolley service then knocked on, cell unlocked and I got tossed a sausage roll and Ts lunch.

I sat watching TV at the desk whilst finishing my food and wondered what was taking T so long as he hadn't come back yet. When he returned he had a spring in his step. He had just had a visit, so must have gone straight from the 2nd day screening to the Visits' Hall.

"Yea, B, my bro and mother came to visit". This baffled me as it was only a few days ago he said he had no family on the outside, but putting that aside I asked him if it was a nice visit. He was monotone in his response, so I didn't ask any other questions.

After he finished his lunch, the guard came back for T as he had not finished all the tests required by the nurse. Moments later the door opened yet again, and in walks Bobby. "I'm back, let's get smelly bollox outa here".

Bobby ruthlessly started pulling off T's bedsheets and stuffing T's belongings into a clear bin bag. Turns out

Brett's cousin had just arrived at the wing and they want to bunk up together, so Bobby took the opportunity to come back with me. Bobby knew the guard and had a quiet word and the move was confirmed and T is moving down to the noisy bottom floor! Suits me fine!

It cracked me up to watch Bobby, without any respect, flinging T's worldly goods into a bag like he just didn't care and dumped the bag of crap outside the cell and got the guard to lock the door behind him like that took care of business.

"Man, can't you smell it in here, I could smell it across the landing". Well, to be honest, I must have gone nose blind from spending 2 days in a room locked up with the smelly samurai-wielding no family, yet family come on visit, conspiracy theorist T!

Bobby started straight away with his deep clean ritual. By the time he had finished cleaning like a mad man, I could taste the chemicals, but the cell was spotless and clean. He sat on the desk whilst I got on writing my book and he turned to me all giddy and said, "I got some rice and a day out". I didn't know what the hell that meant but sounded good! I said, "Rice as in egg fried rice, and a day out as in you've got release or a hospital visit?" Bobby pissed himself with laughter at how unstreet savvy I was.

"Rice is spice. We call it rice should the screws hear you say it. Yo that rice last night was banging, when you're actually referring to spice". Spice being a synthetic drug, like a cheap and dangerous version of cannabis. I was intrigued firstly by what it looked like and secondly how he got it in here.

He had a rummage in the bin and dug out some of the grease proof sleeve that the sausage roll came out of and had made himself a hand rolled cigarette. I said, "Is that it ?", pointing to the tobacco that was rolled in the middle of it. "No mate, that's the baccy, this is the spice" as he handed me a corner of an A4 piece of paper. I thought he was having a laugh at my expense.

It was scentless and would be undetectable with the human eye. It was a piece as big as a thumbnail which he was ripping into smaller pieces distributed evenly into his 'Rollie'.

It is smuggled into prison to whoever is dealing it on the wing via letter sent in from the outside. Usually disguised as some type of love letter but laced in spice which is soaked then dried into the paper.

When smoked, it will give you a more intense high than a cannabis joint. I wondered how he was going to light it as the prison was now a smoke free prison, so any prisoners who wished to get their nicotine fix would need to buy an E-cigarette or vape pen which Bobby already had. The ban also covered lighters and anyone found with one could get extra time added to their sentence. "Watch this" Bobby said standing up clutching an empty fluid capsule that goes inside the E-Cig. He pulled out the chair, put the capsule underneath, levered it forward then slammed it back down with force like a makeshift guillotine. The capsule ping ponged around the cell. It took him about 10 attempts with each funnier than the last and with each making Bobby more frustrated and shouting obscenities at the capsule going missing.

Finally, with one finally slam, the plastic part that would normally hold the nicotine liquid popped off leaving a round, small metal connector that screws into the E-cig. That's exactly what Bobby did, the filament which would normally heat the liquid was now exposed and glowing orange and was just about hot enough to light up his rice joint! The timing couldn't have come any better as Bobby definitely needed to chill out after that little workout.

The smoke billowed under my nostrils and it smelt very similar to a joint of cannabis. He switched on the tv and turned up prison radio and started dancing round the cell like a gangster whilst MC'ing. It kept me amused for about an hour, listening to lyrics like "I get out my gats while the bitch is on her back", which translated means he is holding his guns whilst having sex. The things he came out with to the beat did tickle me! "I'm Bobby, you can't touch me, I'm the best there ever be, ill sting like a bee and I'm with my boy Daniel." It was nice to be included in his lyrics, what a lovely gesture being counted in such high regard in his drug and weapons filled rhymes.

All of a sudden, he would drop to the floor, and concerned I'd peer over the bed to find him spontaneously doing 50 pushups! 3pm came, with the spice wearing off, boredom set in and Bobby chewing on slices of bread that he'd stored up, it was time for a meltdown.

CHAPTER 6. ICE CREAM SHOP FOR DRUGGIES

In the prison, filled with inmates that have all come in with drink and drug addictions, the prison accommodates their needs with substitutes to keep the peace. Diazepam for cocaine addicts and alcoholics, Subutex for heroin addictions and crack, Methadone for heroin users, a concoction of pain killers like Codeine, Co-codamol and Pregabalin, all served from a small door acting like an ice cream shop for druggies. People have clearly done this before and know how to lay the system when they come in to get prescribed the drugs or fake it so they can then sell them on.

People would pretend to swallow them at the meds hatch in front of the nurse, when really they were hiding them under their tongue. Once out of sight, spit into a tissue to dry off and either keep for later or sell them on.

Bobby, who formerly used heroine and smoked crack on the outside of prison, was prescribed with Methadone and was clucking for his next fix. The guards let only a few prisoners from each level out at a time to go and queue for their drugs. From our door window you could see the queue forming, which was enough to send Bobby over the edge. Like a gorilla in a cage that had been cattle prodded, he started shouting at the guards through the hinges of the door. "Yo Gov", and repeated this process until the guard finally got bored of hearing it and came over. "Come on, man, open up, I need my meth before dinner and I can see people down there". The guard replied, "They're from level 2. There's too many people down there at the moment, as soon as 2s are done we will call 3s." Bobby was fuming and punched the door like a boxing bag over and over.

I saw a totally different side to this easy going, take it all in his stride, Bobby. He obviously had a dark side due to the addiction and craving for drugs. "That guy's a waste man, I want my fucking drugs! Wouldn't do this on the outside, being denied my medication. They are doing this on purpose, taking the piss, fuck this shit, I can't have them after dinner as it makes me feel sick. They don't wanna see me flip, I'll knock them all out as soon as they open the doors". He made his way back to the door and started thumping and banging and kicking and shouting. "What the fuck man, I NEED MY DRUGS," he muttered over and over to himself during the pasting of the cell door which, luckily, was made of metal.

As I sat there, I finally realised why and what type of people were door bangers that I heard all night; I was witnessing it live for myself. He was physically crawling over the door and frame whilst constantly updating me on how many people were in the queue and how much of a liberty it was that he was not allowed to get his drugs on his terms. He'd stand, he'd sit, he'd chill out and then do the whole process all over again.

Finally, the stress, emotion and anxiety got too much and he pressed the emergency bell. Emergency bell it was not, it took a good 15 minutes before they came to peer through the door to see what the actual emergency was. Bobby spewed it all out in an extremely aggressive manner, and to diffuse the situation the guard relented and opened to cell door for him to go and join the queue.

Bobby changed instantly from a mad man to a courteous gentleman, thanking the guard as he squeezed past him and the cell door and profusely apologising for his rant. The cell was locked behind him, finally a minute's peace.

He came back an hour later, a completely different person. He was buzzing and bubbly again, full of life and told me the stories of his adventures over the past hour; that he'd had a cup of tea round Brett's, talked to some mates through their locked door and got more drugs from his dealer passed underneath the cell door.

Time for dinner, 4:30pm, and we were let out last which means the dregs and even more dried food than normal from the heat lamps. There wasn't much choice, vegetable cottage pie and potatoes, it was that or lamb stew.

Back in the cell, I had to use the bread to make a cottage pie sandwich with not being a fan of vegetables. It was the only way to make it palatable enough to get it down so I wouldn't be hungry tonight.

The rest of the afternoon into early evening consisted of watching awful Tv programmes about antiques, pawn shops and improving houses and watching Bobby clean the cell yet again, which seemed to be a daily habit. He would spray everything in bleach which just stuck to the back of my throat and gave me breathing difficulties and a headache.

6pm was Simpsons, followed by a heart-breaking phone call to the wife. It just hurt to hear her voice which you could hear she was hurting too. So nice to talk to her, though, and Tess, and hearing about their day, but so painful ending the call and back to the loneliness feeling.

Thoughts about being home with them and not in this rotting, inadequate, claustrophobic and uncomfortable cell filled my head. It was the first-time reality hit me, like a ton of bricks.

I'd done a few days, done pretty much the same thing every day so far, nothings changed, days turn to nights, sleep, wake and then do the same again. Just trying to do things to pass and kill time, that's it. Mundane, boring, less than basic conditions and caged like an animal, it's going to be groundhog day every day for 2 and a half years.

Each day goes by, the stronger the feeling of love for my wife and child at home. They say absence makes the heart grow fonder, never has that saying felt so true. 4 days in, feeling like a month, I still can't grasp the fact that I've still got hundreds and hundreds and hundreds of days left. For the sake of my mentality and sanity, I don't know if I want to, or should do, try to get my head round it.

People's comments that prison is like a holiday camp are far from reality.

Wednesday came, with 2 things different from normal. Firstly, Bobby decided to have his day out. He'd mentioned it on Monday but from his large portion of rice, MC battle and dance off, decided to save his so called 'day out' until today. This should be interesting.

Bobby, leaving on Monday, had forfeited his canteen to the guy in the next cell who came in for a light of his makeshift tea bag spice loaded joint. It absolutely stank the cell out like burnt paper, burnt tea leaves, chemical and spice. Another reason he came in was so he could order £12 of items from Bobby's canteen sheet in return for 4 Pregabalin pills which were worth £4 each. Down the hatch they went, followed by some of his E-cig bong which was rammed with spice paper rather than E-Cig liquid.

Within a few minutes his eyes were glazed from the cocktail of the 2 drugs hitting his system. It sent Bobby loopy, he bounced around the cell like a Tasmanian Devil. I saw the Riverdance, a spontaneous strip show, a boxing match with only one person in the ring and a loop of whoop whooping. He would stop every few minutes to tell me he was clucking, ask me if his eyes looked glazed and do I think he is mental. Then continue.

Lunch came, coronation chicken baguettes, biscoffee biscuits and a yoghurt. Bobby couldn't get it in his mouth quick enough before chasing it down with a pint of water, jumping up to the top bunk and was asleep almost instantly. I guess this is why he calls it his day out as he was asleep for the remainder of the day.

After lunch I heard something being shoved underneath the cell door. It was post, such a welcoming sight. It was a letter from Hannah which she had posted about 4 days ago. With Bobby comatose above me, I lay on my bed and prepared to take the time to read it slowly, thoroughly and take in each word whole heartedl,, reading the words I could envisage the words as though she was here reading it to me.

The letter was deep and full of feelings. She was shocked at my sentence length and how much she cried when she got the call from my solicitor. I struggled to read, line by line, through my blurred teary eyes which were rolling down my cheeks.

The words of love, support and that she would wait for me even if I got a life sentence was just what I wanted to hear. Yet at the same time it cut me deep, and I had to take breaks between paragraphs to find the strength to read on. There was also an attachment, Hannah had written a page of various quotes of strength and love topically about being apart and still being in love. It was just the content that I needed at the right time to make me feel settled.

I immediately wrote a response pledging my love, how I missed them dearly and how we will have a happy normal family life after this is over.

The rest of the day consisted of writing this book, poor daytime tv until dinner time. Bobby woke, ate (lamb stew and rice) then went back to enjoying his day out.

7pm came and someone was banging their door down across the landing, double what the normal door banging beat was and he howled like a demented fox and held the note for as long as possible. It went on until 8pm when I heard the guards' alarm and whistles go off, heavy footfall followed, and they all tried to pile into the cell. It was a bottle neck as 6 guards eagerly stood outside the cell unable to squeeze in. You could smell a weird smell like burnt hair mixed with weed creep underneath the door. The guy somehow had managed to set alight to his cell.

I wouldn't have cared as much if I wasn't locked behind a heavily locked door and unable to escape should the flames engulf the wing. The feelings were awful of the helplessness should something like that actually happen, as I'd be in my own little personal oven.

With all the commotion, Bobby was still comatose, and I began to get a pain in my stomach. It had been 5 days since I'd had a proper poo and I think it was time! Looking at the metal throne with no toilet seat covered in pee stains, piss and pubes and not even been able to see the bottom due to the rust was not inviting. I got a tissue and water and gave it a wipe down before trying to levitate unsuccessfully before just plonking on the metal rim.

Not only was it uncomfortable from the thick metal putting pressure into my leg but also the thought anyone walking by could look in at me sitting there doing my business was so off-putting. Bobby's head also being about a foot away from where I was perched made this experience extremely degrading, embarrassing and inhumane.

I squeezed, I pushed, I strained but all I could pass was 1 lousy rabbit dropping despite the stomach pain. On the verge of sweating and giving birth to my heart, I gave up!

The evening was pretty much a replica of the previous one, apart from Iron Man being the film of choice tonight which kept me entertained for a few hours.

CHAPTER 7. ALLADINS CAVE OF CONTRABAND

Friday came, and it was canteen day and library day, but not before some drama on the wing. Phones in jail are like a bullion bar of gold. A small Chinese phone the size of your thumb can be smuggled in via the rectum with a little help with some olive oil, or you could grease up a guard to bring one in. They can sell on the wing for between £350 and £500.

I often wondered how you can pay for something like that on £11 a week prison money but you call your people on the outside to transfer to a designated account number and once received, then they will hand over the goods, if you're lucky.

iphones are also up for sale from £700-£1000, but if you get caught with one and especially if it has a camera you could get up to 1 extra year added to your sentence. With E wing being the induction wing it was like an Aladdin's cave of contraband that you could get your hands on from people freshly bringing things into the prison purposely to sell. £200 for 30 grams of tobacco, heroine or crack at £50 for half a gram, spice £80 for an A4 sheet or £20 for a credit card size and also an abundance of pills was on offer.

Someone new on the wing had let slip that they smuggled in a mobile and it was inevitable being in a jail full of opportunists and thieves that it wasn't long before the news spread like wildfire. The phone got stolen.

There are 2 main unwritten rules in prison. Firstly, you don't grass on each other. Secondly, you don't steal from each other or from other people's cells.

It took no time at all before word got round who the culprit was. The doors were opened about 8:30am, and I showered, walked round the yard and made my way back to the cell just before bang up when you could hear screaming from the ground floor. Everyone looked over the balcony directly underneath us.

A kettle of boiling water and sugar had been thrown over the phone thief as punishment for stealing the phone. We were all pushed back into our cells and locked up to stop it escalating and out our door window you could just make out the guards carrying both those involved out of the wing like a battering ram, with the prisoner being carried in the middle horizontally between about 8 guards.

Noodles and cheese came round for lunch and Bobby went on to carry on with another day out which he initiated after the commotion on the wing. The guard came to the door and shouted "Library" and, I jumped at the opportunity to do something different. "Yes, mate", I said, and the door opened and he told me to go wait at the bottom of the wing. He managed to rally 15 library goers together which was apparently quite rare for E wing.

Like a bunch of tourists following a leader, we went through one locked gate after another, trekked through different wings of the prison and eventually, I was stood outside. We walked round the perimeter of the grim Victorian building to another equality grim looking Victorian building.

Inside, however, and to my surprise, was a fully-fledged library. It made me feel slightly normal again, and for a split second I wasn't in prison anymore, I was a normal citizen in a normal library.

I scoured the books on offer from sci-fi, biographies to fiction before finding some newspapers, a nice comfy chair and just enjoyed the time out the cell and mentally, out of prison. 30 minutes flew by before the guard rounded us up like a herd of sheep to escort us back to the wing. I didn't get a book in the end but that didn't matter, I thoroughly enjoyed killing 45 minutes in a different environment to the stale, uneasy, boring atmosphere of the wing and not being locked in the cell.

It was 11am and there was a guard waiting outside my cell. "Mr Hockey? You got a visit, get your ID card." Bobby was still asleep so I grabbed my ID card rather excitedly and nervous all at the same time and overwhelmed about how we would all take seeing each other for the first time in over a week. To be able to finally hold my wife and show her I'm actually ok, regardless of the god-awful conditions and grotty people.

I got led off the wing to a holding cell with about 10 other inmates. One was bragging to another about getting 10 years for a Class A drugs case and shooting someone in the face and how his plane was stormed by armed officers when he came back from Dubai, the sentence didn't really reflect the crime so I could tell it was just a blag to sound impressive to everyone else in the room, but you got to just let them play their card however they want in prison, people can be whoever they want and you just need to let them.

Eventually, after an uncomfortable and anxious 30 minutes wait, the door opened, and we were called one by one by name to go for a pat down search, given a stinky orange bib and entered the Visits' Hall.

To my left was a central station where I handed over my ID card and was told which table number to head to. The hall was already filled with visitors already seated. I scanned the room to try and locate my family and spotted the wife stood up towards the back. I couldn't get over to her quick enough and she fell into my arms with excitement, and she smothered me with kisses whilst my mum remained seated.

After a long embrace, she whispered in my ear to give my Mum some attention as she was quite delicate and struggling with the whole experience. Mum stood up and as soon as we hugged, she burst into tears which was heartbreaking to see your own mother with uncontrollable tears rolling down her face. As she sat down, she was still crying, they sat on the opposite side of the table and I grabbed one of each of their hands and held tight like I didn't ever want to let go.

It was bizarre to sit in front of the people that you'd been thinking about all week and now they are there right in the flesh, very surreal. Even though it had only been one week, it felt like so much longer. We kept repeating that I shouldn't be in here and looking round at others, they said I stuck out like a sore thumb and don't fit in or suit this lifestyle, the worst comment was that they wished I could come back with them but we both know that wouldn't happen for years yet and it was devastating and to physically see them both in pain was soul destroying. We all tried to put on a brave face and I tried to reassure them both that this wasn't as violent or dangerous as stereotypically everyone thinks it is, just more boring than anything and it seemed to settle them slightly.

Hannah looked more beautiful that I could ever remember in my own head. She had dyed her hair darker and I forgot how big her breasts were and couldn't keep my eyes off them! I showered her in compliments and said how much I've missed and love her. As she sat there (after a 3-hour journey to get here from the south) I just felt so lucky to have such a pretty, strong and supportive wife whilst we go through this traumatic time together.

Mum had brought a handful of change to spend on the vending machines and went to get me some goodies which I had to consume whilst in the visit hall, as nothing could be taken back. Me and Hannah got into a deeper conversation about our love for one another and how we will get through this, we had quite a few more passionate kisses over the table till my mother returned.

She brought coke, crisps, chocolate, it felt like Christmas. The initial taste of coke was like an explosion of sugar in my mouth. It was ecstasy! Mum and Hannah filled me in about what had been going on outside, updates on other family members and how Tess was coping. Turns out she wasn't. She was sleep walking, waking up crying, screaming "Daddy" during the night, crying to mummy during the day that she missed our family days, me putting her to bed and reading her stories. Her teacher had called to state she had noticed a change in Tess's behavior at school and after being informed of the situation by my wife, counselling has now been offered. The news hit me like a spade to the face, I felt absolutely awful how others were suffering indirectly as a result of me being imprisoned and there was nothing I could do.

We got about 40 minutes in total, but it felt like 10, when they shouted "Finish up" and started to usher people out of the room. I hugged my Mum first and she was inconsolable. Next, I held my wife so tight whispering in her ear of my undying and unconditional love before getting a final kiss and being told to take a seat. All prisoners needed to remain seated as the visitors made their way out of the hall.

Watching them walk out the back of the hall getting their final waves in and mouthing love you, I blew a final kiss myself and that was it, they were gone, I was crushed. Sitting there as the silence fell in the room, I was in a state of shock, destroyed on the inside and on the verge of what felt like a breakdown, I sat and took deep breaths to try and contain myself and to not lose it completely in front of everyone.

Looking around the hall at the other 30-odd prisoners, all looked as equally shell shocked and then, row by row, the tables were called to return to their cells. We were all heavily patted down from head to toe exiting the hall, checking for any contraband that may have been concealed and passed from visitors.

Back at the cell, Bobby was awake and eating whatever had been delivered from lunch, I felt slightly high from the mammoth sugar intake, and sadness turned to excitement as I recited the whole visit to Bobby, about how enjoyable it was and hard at the same time. He sympathised with me and said it was always hard during visits, that's why he decides not to have visitors at all whilst in prison, he can't deal with it mentally.

Just seeing them for a minute would have just meant the world to me, a moment of normality and physical contact with my wife and to talk to my mother was such a welcome break and well timed as my first week had started to take its toll.

Our heart to heart was cut short when the delivery of canteen was brought to the door. It was goods shrink wrapped in a thick clear plastic bag which was everything that Bobby had ordered in exchange for the Pregabalins. Inside was Nutella, peanut butter, baby oil, chocolate, biscuits, sugar and shampoo. Ensuring nothing was missing, Bobby kept his foot in the door whilst quickly checking his shopping list against the items delivered.

One vital and very important and expensive item was missing, the vape capsules! I heard every swearword that had ever been created. "Someone's stolen them", he claimed, and expletives turned to desperation as he tried to convince the guard he needs them for medical reasons and is dying for a smoke but this is the only thing that helps cut the craving whilst he tries to give up. The story was a crock of shit, the reality is he owed these to the drug dealer and had already taken the pills on his day out.

You could see the panic on Bobby's face as the guard said there was nothing he could do but get a refund for him to go on next week's canteen and slammed the door behind him.

An hour went by hearing the injustice as he paced the cell before pushing the "room service" button once again. He played the guards like a fiddle as a different one came to answer the bell. "The other guard said he would replace the lost vapes over an hour ago, he went to get them from reception and never came back".

Bobby was crafty, and from all the years being behind bars knew all the tips and tricks. He knew there were vapes at Reception ready for people when they came in on arrival. That could be the solution to his vape capsule conundrum. The guard said he would chase it up, and after another hour another guard arrived with the capsules. Result!

Bobby was as happy and excited with the win as a kid at Xmas. Firstly, resolving his issue with the drug dealer and secondly, that his plan actually worked and getting one up on the 'screws'.

The evening consisted of another disgusting dinner, Bobby getting his hands on a sleeping pill and him being dead to the world for the rest of the night.

I called the wife and daughter to say I was missing them, to hear their voices and to tell them how much I loved them. The phone started to bleep at me so I knew it was due to cut off, whilst relaying the information to Hannah, it cut off completely. I was frantically trying to call her back, but the system doesn't let you call in such quick succession.

I remember a poster on the wall on how to check the balance; 118# followed by your pin. "You have 0 Pence". I was distraught, helpless and with no way to tell Hannah of the phone situation. I sat on my bed and thought about it all night. It's amazing how little things you take for granted, like being able to just pick up the phone to speak to someone when you want to compared to now being cut off and having no phone credit, was agonising.

Saturday morning came, and underneath the door 2 canteen sheets had been posted. My first time that I can actually order some luxury goods whilst in prison. It was so exciting. I sat and stared at every item, carefully choosing with a small balance exactly what I needed. I ordered ketchup, biscuits, orange juice, apple and blackcurrant juice, Weetabix, brown sauce, salt and a cheap happy shopper Redbull replica.

After that excitement, I was still affected by my phone dilemma which I referred to my prison guru for help. Bobby said there was an app for emergency phone credit and once filled in and signed off, it should go in on the same day.

As soon as the doors opened, I rushed downstairs to beat the queue, grabbed the app, ran back to my cell, filled it out and rushed out to get a guard to sign it off. It was such a relief. The app said it would take £5 out of your prison account which is made up of the money I brought into prison, plus the prison system gives you 50p a day top up into your account which is good for people who don't have any money to put in their account. But they also take £1.50 per week back off your account for TV and Electricity! In one hand, out the other.

Bobby had another 'Day Out' which was nice as I felt I had the cell to myself with him out the way tucked up in bed. It was only a matter of days left for him now till his release date, so another day of sleep is another day closer.

After bang-up, I left it for only an hour before religiously checking the phone. I developed an OCD of punching in the 118# plus my pin, hoping that the credit had been put on. Sunday was a replica of the day before and still no phone credit to my frustration. I started to get anxious about Bobby leaving tomorrow, knowing I would either get a new cell mate or be moved to a different wing completely. With Bobby making the induction to prison life as painless as possible for me and getting into a routine together that worked for both of us and despite his craziness, drug addiction and anger issues, his heart was in the right place and we clicked. Next, I could get a prisoner that doesn't speak a word of English, ruin my routine, be a door banger, mental or worse, a big crazy killer.

I shouldn't have got as attached and comfortable to having Bobby around as much as I did and knew the day was coming, just didn't realise it would revert me back to that feeling of day 1 in prison all over again.

Monday came, I was stood on the landing waiting for the inevitable. 9am, when an officer came, asked for Bobby, went into the cell. Bobby came out, shook my hand, said "Bye, take care of yourself", and that was it, he was gone. I felt empty, alone and the prison felt overwhelming again.

I went back into the cell ready for bang up. Once locked in, the biggest bonus of being alone was finally being able to go to the toilet by myself, relax and relieve myself from the stomach pains, embarrassment of poo'ing in front of someone and gain a little bit of dignity back.

I kept pacing the cell, jumping up from the bed every time I heard a guard or keys jingle outside my cell. I paced, I checked the phone, I did pushups, checked the phone some more, paced some more, watched crappy daytime tv and repeated the process until dinner time came. Spring rolls and rice, but whilst standing at the serving hatch I caught a glimpse of one cheeseburger frying at the back, I asked the worker but he said it was for them. I joked around that it was like a mirage and a little piece of heaven even seeing it there at the back. I think he felt sorry for me, quickly put it in a bun and dumped it on my plate. I couldn't believe my luck.

Back in the cell alone, I set out the desk like a table for one at the restaurant so I could enjoy every single bit of this gifted luxurious burger. It tasted like the best burger I had ever put in my mouth. each bite better than the last, I chewed slowly whilst in total tune with my taste buds until it was gone. Don't get me wrong, it was no gourmet burger, completely cheap meat and full of lips and bums but at that exact moment, heaven!

9pm came. I knew most prison vans would have come from the courts by now so looked like I had the cell to myself, so I watched a film then went to bed before midnight without Bobby breathing in the room snoring his head off from his drug induced coma. It was by far the best sleep I've had in prison so far.

Tuesday came and I started to get used to having the cell to myself, thinking I'd actually prefer it just me regardless of having no company. The day started in the normal way. Banging, shouting, cell doors slamming and its only 6am! I tried to get back to sleep but there was enough noise to wake the dead. The breakfast pack I got handed with my dinner last night actually contained something different to porridge oats - Cocopops!

I would have enjoyed them more if it wasn't for the warm UHT milk and having to eat out of a well-used small plastic prison issue blue bowl like a child, along with a white plastic spoon. Afterwards, another chance for a poo in peace, a few laps round the yard, then locked up for the day at 10am. Lots of new faces on the wing now and I no longer felt like the newbie even though I've only been here for just over a week.

It was so hot in the cell and provided a good opportunity to wash my clothes. I blocked the sink with the sandwich bag that breakfast came in, added some shampoo from the free sachets they give us and added the weeks dirty clothes.

Anywhere I could, I hung the garments. The cell looked like a launderette with boxers, socks, t-shirts and trousers hanging up everywhere.

I cleaned the cell, wrote letters and more of this book, then carried on watching tv until 8pm. I could hear keys outside the door; this was it, new cell mate time! I stood up, turned the light on and got ready to stamp my authority on the cell if need be. The door opened, an English guy, late 20's and quite muscley walked in, you could tell this guy worked out.

I stuck out my hand, introduced myself and he responded, 'Jake'. Jake looked far too preppy and well-spoken for prison, it was as if the royal family had dropped off one of their own to give them a taste of prison life experience and I thought I didn't fit in! He looked shell shocked, worse than I probably looked when I arrived and that's saying something.

He didn't even make his bed, just sat on the top bunk. First off, he was relieved that I was his first cell mate and willing to help him in any way I could, the same reception that Bobby gave me. Secondly, he fired a thousand questions at me, exactly the same as I did to Bobby when I arrived.

10pm, I had answered all his initial worries about jail life; from showers, violence, what it's like when the door opens, the yard and prison food. He had come to prison totally unprepared and totally unexpected.

After a boozy night out about 6 months earlier, he'd got into a fight and the other guy came worse off and subsequently he was arrested. A trip to court got him community service (unpaid community work) a small fine and a tag (device attached to his leg to monitor curfews and movements). He was a professional trainer at a gym, but worked late one evening which made him breach his curfew time. He was summoned to court where he expected a bigger fine and an extension to his community work. Instead, he was handed a 7 week prison sentence. No one knew he was in prison so I showed him how to use the phone system. One problem, from Reception to the cell he had lost his phone pin!

He lived at home with his parents and would normally be back there by now and had no way of making contact to let them know of the situation. I felt sorry for him and he was sat there looking at my pictures of my family on the wall and said he was relieved to be in with a family guy and someone like himself as he'd expected everyone to be London gang members.

We talked until midnight and he couldn't believe my story, sentence or how unfair it was on me and specifically my family. Shame he wasn't on my jury bench! We both went to bed feeling comfortable and relieved of the cell mate situation and even made plans for an in-cell workout plan to kill the days.

Chapter 8. IM A CAT C PRISONER

Another 6am wakeup from the sheer noise of the wing, Jake fired a million more questions at me about how to get a pin, pin credit, money sent into prison, how to pass the day for the other 23 hours that we are locked up. At 8am I was still answering his questions when a female guard appeared at the door. "Mr Hockey" she shouted through the gap. "Get your stuff, you're moving to Trinity". Trinity was the prison's equivalent wing to a Cat C Prison. I was ecstatic and scared at the same time. I'd just got my 3rd cell mate of the week and now I'm just about to go and meet the 4th. She said she would be back in 30 mins to do the move. Jake looked stunned! At least he had a few hours' crash course introduction to prison from me, but I had to put myself first especially as he be out in weeks and I had years left yet.

With all my belongings now confined to 2 cardboard boxes and bedding in a clear bag, it was time to go. A handshake and farewell to Jake, I followed the guard who watched me struggle to balance 2 boxes on top of each other and trailing a bag of heavy bedding behind me. We went through about 5 heavy metal locked gates and through various wings before ending up outside in the rain.

Inside prison, you don't even realize if it's raining outside or not unless it happened to be raining in the yard due to small inaccessible windows in the cell and artificial strip lighting. I welcomed the rain drops on my face and dripping onto my glasses. It was so refreshing to feel a snippet of freedom and leaving that chapter of the induction wing behind. The journey was the same that I made to go to the library, but this time I'm heading inside Trinity wings which means I've been recategorised to C cat status, which means I'm low risk, can now apply for employment and my canteen funds go up slightly from £11 per week to £14.

It was still social time, so all prisoners were out as we headed into the Trinity block. In the middle of the wing there was a cheap small pool table, the same you find in a pub which was crowded by rowdy inmates cheering on or reacting to poorly taken shots. It seemed everyone stopped what they were doing to take in and size up the newbie on the wing.

Walking through, I had numerous people approaching me and asking if I had various items in my boxes from towels to jumpers or what drugs I'd brought into prison. I had to kindly decline each request as I walked through the lion's den and into the safety of the guard's office.

I watched on whilst the guards picked out vacancies in certain cells whilst discussing amongst themselves my compatibility with the madmen that were contained within, hence while their cells were one man light! They finally narrowed it down to 2 which they thought be the best of a bad bunch. Lovely! "Follow me to the next room where you can wait". This room was an old cell that had clearly been trashed, all fixtures and fittings had been removed, no light, strong odor of piss and even the light had been smashed out.

Other prisoners peered in like I was some kind of freak show looking through the punched-out window in the cell door. 10 mins later the door reopened and the game of follow the leader resumed.

Up 4 flights of stairs to the 4th floor, passing people on each floor peering over the landing to where I was ending up. "G429, this is you Mr Hockey". He opened the door and I was just about to walk in, heart pounding, when the guard backed out the cell. "Not this one, apparently he is classed as high risk due to drug and alcohol abuse. Stay there and I'll go sort it in the office".

The cell was relocked and I'm now just stood in the middle of the landing, 4th floor, surrounded by my boxes and bags and looking like a tit with everyone staring at me. One guy was desperate to get my attention, hollering "Oi Mate, OI MATE" over and over until I eventually made eye contact. The usual questions followed, what you in for, how long you got, then he reassured me "You be glad you not been put in with him mate, he's high risk I think". Lovely, just what I wanted to hear!

I could hear frantic tapping behind me. The guy from the cell I was meant to go in with was at the door with his top off, shaved head apart from a pineapple looking top knot, trying to get my attention with his face pressed against the window. "You alright yea." Not checking on my welfare, more of a vetting process asking if I'm actually alright as in a decent character. "Yes mate, I'm good," I replied with a hint of sarcasm. He then held something up and flashed it quickly in the window before making it disappear out of sight. "Will this be an issue ?" I was completely taken by surprise and intrigued to finally see with my own eyes an IPHONE 5! How did he get it, why is he so calmly informing me and what are the consequences going to be should you get caught with one, and if I'm in the same cell will they think it's mine. It was very surreal to see an inmate with an iphone. Before I could even answer the guard came back "He was blagging, mate, trying to stop me putting you in with him to keep a single. This is your cell, Mr Hockey." Door unlocked, in I went.

Like the first day at school again, and going through the same introductory process I had done with 3 cell mates previous ensued.

His name was Garrison, 24, white, 6ft tall and skinny build. Quite a geezer and was in for drug dealing. He apologised for the initial issue and reassured me it wasn't me; he was just trying a blag to keep a single cell for a bit. His previous cell mate had moved out a week ago and sold the phone onto him and had been enjoying facetime phone sex with his Mrs ever since.

Whilst making the top bunk, we exchanged stories about what we were in for, family and the lengths of our own sentences. He got busted on a police sting for delivering 16 bags of cocaine via mopeds. After a roadblock stopped him in his tracks he was arrested. He pleaded Not Guilty to get bail to buy him some more time to pay off other dealers he owed money to and ended up breaching his tag conditions too, which got him another 8 months, and has served 4 months so far of a 5-and-a-half-year sentence.

As horrible as it sounded, it made me feel more comfortable about my own sentence being with someone who will serve longer than me for once. We settled in for the night sharing stories of family, our partners on the outside and watched Lord of the Rings together. Well, I seemed to be the only one watching as Garrison sat there texting his bird the whole time.

It actually put me on edge how brazen he was with the phone and any guard walking by would easily be able to spot the glow on his face, so I eventually crawled up to the top bunk and fell asleep with the tv on in the background.

I woke up first. It was so much less noisy on G wing than it was on E and managed to sleep in until 8am. I was bursting for a wee but didn't want to wake Garrison with the toilet literally being behind his head so I sat and looked round the room. It felt slightly more homely with shelves on the wall, cupboards and condiments already stocked on the side and pictures of Garrison's bird and mates on the wall next to the TV which had been stuck on with toothpaste and plastic bucket seats under the desk. Unfortunately, the bed was still as uncomfortable as the last cell. Only benefit is this bunk was a wooden frame instead of metal, at least the squeak of the metal frame every time someone moved had gone.

I couldn't hold it anymore and climbed down and inevitably woke Garrison up. "Morning Mate, was on phone late last night Facetime the Mrs so I'm going back to bed for a bit." I asked if he minded if I stuck the tv on in the background, but he just reached under the bed, handed me the remote and turned over. I'll take that as a no you don't mind then!

Holding the remote, I smiled inside; we actually had a remote! in the last cell, we had to physically get up and do everything by hand using the buttons on the tv, as remotes were like rocking horse shit in E wing. From the top of my bunk, I could freely flick from one channel to the other, the novelty of a remote was amazing.

8:30am, the door opened, and I noticed on this door there was a metal knob on the inside so you could lock it or unlock it yourself (once the guard had unlocked the door) to stop people just walking into your cell. On the landing there seemed to be a lot less guards standing around than E wing, I'm guessing because it's meant to be a Cat C wing, with more trusted prisoners than B Cat.

I spotted the phone on the wall at the bottom floor of the wing and immediately tried to call home. By now I'd got used to the pin phone code from constantly calling every day for a week, and I punched in the numbers like a flash and was so excited and buzzing to tell Hannah the news. "Hello." Just to hear her voice always filled me with relief and sadness at the same time. "Baby, they've finally added credit and they've moved me".

We spent the full 5 minute limit talking about how hard it's been, not speaking to each other, had she received my letters, how Tess was coping and how much we loved and missed each other. As the phone beeped, Hannah was still crying from being heartbroken knowing I'm in here, finding it hard alone on the outside and how much she loved me dearly and we'd repeat "love you, love you, love you" before the phone cuts out.

I just stood there with the handset in my hand, stunned, finally getting to speak after all this time, her loving supportive words but feeling her pain and hearing her cry was a knife to the heart.

"EXERCISE!" a guard shouted from the other side of the wing. Rather than going back into the cell and waking Garrison, I followed the herd from G wing, through the gates to K wing and out the door to the yard.

It was different from E wing yard. It had 6 raised flower beds on the left, some outside gym equipment like you'd find at a park and on the right, some temporary office cabins and full netting overhead to stop things being thrown over from the outside.

People were still walking round anticlockwise and in ethnic groups. Head held high, chest puffed out, I started my laps. I felt like everyone was staring at me, sizing me up, knew I was the new guy with Trinity being a place for people with longer sentences, but it could just be psychological and in reality probably no one even noticed me.

After an hour with many laps, soaked up the sun and a few reps on the gym equipment I headed back in. I was looking forward to getting to know Garrison a bit better and becoming accustomed to my new cell. Walking back into the cell, he had only just got out of bed as they locked the door behind me.

With the tv on in the background I sat on the bottom bunk to chat with Garrison who sat nearest the door. He had put his dressing gown over the corner of the top of the bunk to drape down and cover the view from the door window where he sat. I started to ask questions to spark a conversation, but he would only pay me part attention whilst he continued to text. I'd find myself repeating the same question two or three times before giving up.

Lunch came around 11:30 and I took the opportunity to climb back to the top bunk to watch tv and leave him to his text marathon. Just when I thought he was being too brazen with the phone ("Hello mate, yeah got a new pad mate, he's alright, yeah man I miss the craziness of B wing"), he jumped up and headed behind the shower curtain hung from the ceiling which partly concealed the toilet from the bunk.

I felt so nervous and apprehensive sat there whilst he blatantly had a full-blown conversation and all it took was a peer in or to hear it whilst walking by and our cell would be spun and unknown consequences for something that wasn't my fault. What if they thought the phone was mine or he was to blame me for it?

Garrison wasn't the only one on the wing with a phone. It seemed to be a common practice for other prisoners in various wings to have phones as Garrison would also Facetime other people on the wing. Every 30 minutes he would go and part charge the phone behind the tv. The prisons hadn't really thought it through. In the changeover from smoking prisons to nonsmoking prisons, E-cigs and vape pens were introduced as a replacement and to charge them you had to do so via USB, which they included the plug with the device. Perfect for prisoners to use with their USB phone charger cable.

Every time I'd hear keys pass the cell my heart would skip a beat. Garrison was so carefree with it, I worried for both of us! Every time I climbed down to the toilet, I'd get a brief conversation where he would peel himself away from the phone. Sometimes he wouldn't even be texting and instead would be on YouTube or playing cards online. I did ask Garrison his take on getting caught with the phone, and he responded stating that if he gets another month or so on top of his sentence, he would rather take the hit and have the luxury of having the phone, for however long that may be.

Apparently even though the guideline is up to 12 months if you get caught with a phone, most people who have been found with a phone got only an extra 1 month added to their sentence. He did add that if he got caught it might be longer for him as he already had an 18-day extension for being caught drunk on the wing on hooch (prison made vodka). I asked how he got caught being drunk. He said the stuff he took was like pure alcohol and he was slurring his words, slumped over the pool table and being abusive to the guards. Garrison doesn't do subtlety, obviously!

With Bobby, the art of conversation and using the time to bond, swap stories and comment on whatever was happening, but with Garrison I felt redundant and replaced by a phone to keep him company.

Being in a concrete cell, prisoners had to get creative to win the game of hide and seek against the officers to conceal items. It wasn't often that they spun cells (checked the cell for contraband) due to not having enough staff and the majority of the time it was intelligence led (other prisoners grassing on you).

Old school prisoners still used the old technique of hiding it in the prison pocket (rectum). New school prisoners were not so willing so had became inventive. Some put the phone in a latex glove then hid it in the middle of their E45 cream tub they got from Healthcare especially. Another great place was in the water cistern behind the toilet which was unscrewed daily using the nail clippers. Another cut the sole out of his shoe and stashed it in the heel, others cut a hole in their mattress or pillow and stuffed it in the middle. The craftiest was a prisoner who soaked his boxers daily and hung them up to dry on his makeshift washing line. He then stashed the phone in the front crotch pocket, no one ever even thought of looking there and the phone was that small you'd never know. Me and Garrison kicked in the skirting underneath the tv and he hid his phone there and we just put the wood back like nothing ever happened.

Chapter 9. Like a Scene from Oliver

Dinner came, I grabbed my plate and waited outside for Garrison, and we walked down the stairs together and waited for the gates to the servery to be opened. Even outside the cell with no phone, there was no effort to make conversation and we ended up getting separated by other people joining the queue, so after being served I made my own way back to the cell. Spuds and chicken leg tonight, amazing. Feeding time at the zoo always reminded me of a scene out of Oliver! Grown men clinging to blue plastic child size picnic plates and bowls in line waiting for food; the portion size was child's like too. Please sir, I want some more! Then having to go back and eat it with a plastic knife and fork next to the toilet. Grim!

I've never missed home so much and wondered what my girls were up to at home. I gave them a call and it seems that they were feeling exactly the same. Hannah cried down the phone and was struggling and Tess kept asking when I'd be back. I sucked it up to try stay strong for her but was dying on the inside. I felt weak, hurt, homesick and depressed.

Before I knew it, the 5 mins were up, phone beeping, wife still crying and I managed to get in a few last "Llove you's" before it cut off. Back to the cell, lying on my bed alone with thoughts of the call, Hannah, Tess and how many days I had left really overwhelmed me. I was just existing in here. Why me, why is my family having to go through this and how have I been the subject of so much injustice.

The feelings consume me as I lay there motionless until 9pm when Garrison reminded me there was a film on.

Trying to shake the feeling, and another attempt at bonding I got down and sat with him to watch the movie. He was addicted to the phone with constant locking and unlocking the phone, check all inboxes from multiple applications. "Sorry man, mind if I get comfy now?" I took that as "get off my bed, I want to have my own space and privacy with the phone", so I climbed back up to the top bunk where I just fell asleep from sheer boredom.

Friday morning, same routine, doors were unlocked and Garrison stayed in bed. Instead of the normal "Exercise" shout, today I heard "Gym" and went to the bottom floor to check it out. There was a blue door with a locked gate in front of it, and people were waiting with gloves for the weights and sweat towels. I lingered round waiting for it to be opened.

20 of us followed the guard out the door, down some steps to the outside and back into the adjoining building. It was a fully stocked gym, dated machinery but still, it had everything from treadmills, cross trainers, cycles, weights and lots of free weights.

Power walking on the treadmill with a huge incline, was a slice of normality and an hour's break from the humdrum mind-numbing boring morning in the cell. It felt so good, working out, music in the background and the nostalgic feeling of when I used to go the gym before being sentenced.

800 calories burnt off later, back to the wing, quick shower before being slung back into the cell for the day. What

makes today slightly different is my first delivery of canteen.

Shortly after lunch, you could hear the big clear bags containing people's orders being delivered outside of cells. About 30 mins later, a guard would open the door and get you to sign to confirm delivery; it felt like Christmas day. Having ordered a week in advance, I'd forgotten the items that I'd ordered.

The packs of chocolate digestive biscuits and energy drinks got opened immediately. The pot of salt was like seeing a little pot of gold, the difference it will make to mealtimes will be invaluable! And the juice, to not have to drink the plain boring tap water any more was a big relief.

I started putting it all away on the shelves as did Garrison. I felt absolutely robbed when I realised that I'd been charged 69p for ketchup and it was missing from the order. Something so simple felt like such a big deal, although it's only 69p on the outside, with it being about 10% of the money I'd spent, it was a significant amount to lose, including the actual item that I wanted and I'd have to wait another week for the next order to arrive. To say it took me a while to get over it would be an understatement.

The £3 phone credit I put on for the week had also been credited to my delight. Just after I checked, Garrison said "Mate, save your phone credit, call your Mrs from my blower". I was in a moral dilemma; firstly the implications of being caught, how Hannah would feel with me calling her from Garrison's phone and how that phone had replaced me as a cell mate.

Secondly, I get to speak to the Mrs for free, at length and save phone credit! I swallowed my reservations and desperation took over as I grabbed the phone, made my way behind the shower curtain and made the call. She was so happy I called, she cried with happiness. I explained we had longer, and although she was happy for the call, she was also angry at me for putting myself in such a dangerous position, being caught, getting extra time and concerns about getting her into trouble if they found out she willingly took a phone call from a mobile phone from prison.

Whilst on the call, all my senses were on high alert, and I wasn't comfortable on the phone one bit. Any noise, my heart would skip a beat. I spent an hour on the phone and Garrison was giving me signals that he wanted the phone back. Regardless of how naughty it was, I felt liberated. We spoke through so much, more of an in-depth conversation that we have ever had since coming to prison. Garrison laughed at me for being so paranoid, I thanked him for the use of the phone before deleting Hannah's number from the history of the phone, and handed it back.

I went to bed around 12 after watching another film and Garrison spent the majority of the evening doing the normal, glued to his phone. 1:30am, I woke, maybe it was due to the uncomfortable bed or some noise that woke me up, but I could feel the bed slightly vibrating, this is what must have woke me from my slumber.

As I gained consciousness, I could hear a deep but muffled moan coming from below followed by a female orgasm noise coming from a phone. HE WAS BLATENTLY HAVING PHONE SEX WHILST HAVING A TUG IN THE BUNK BELOW!

It made me feel so awkward like I couldn't move or make a sound or get down to have a wee because he was in full session with his Mrs on his iphone" I put my jumper over my head and managed to eventually drift off. How awkward!

Saturday, the same as all other days, up till 9pm, we were looking what was on TV when I made a passing comment about David Haye and Tony Bellew were fighting tonight and how I wish I was at home to watch the boxing match. His face lit up, "I'll get it streaming through my iphone." 5 mins later, there it was, streaming in HD from a link he found on twitter. The phone was sideways, and we both sat there all giddy watching boxing, enjoying it more than normal knowing we shouldn't be watching it and hardly anyone else in the prison would be watching it made it doubly pleasurable to watch the fight. Haye got KO'd in the 5th, but it was amazing to watch it together and we bonded over the fight.

Sunday, I applied for a job at Radio Wanno again to make shows and give information out to other prisons via the Radio Wanno channel on the TV. The job gets you out the cell between 2-4pm each day which would be a welcome break. You also get paid to work, taking your earnings from 50p a day to £1.50 a day. The other rememberable part of the day was our new next-door neighbour, who not only talked to himself all day, decided to turn his cell into a swimming pool tonight. 10pm, it sounded like it was raining inside the wing. I muted the sound, we looked outside and what started as a trickle was now a full-on waterfall from the 4th floor to the bottom. He had kicked the taps off and smashed the feed to the toilet. It excited everyone on the landing who shouted comments such as

"Help I can't swim, I'm drowning" to "Anyone got an umbrella?".

The Guards finally waded their way to the cell. It was all because he got moved onto the wing and didn't want to be on this wing as he had 'Beef' with others on the same wing. The guards shouted, "Tough shit mate, you're staying in there for the night". Turned off his water and left. In the morning there was bed blankets all over the wing on the floors in an attempt to soak up the water. It was flooded and dangerous to walk anywhere as people slipped like an ice rink.

He obviously got his own way as I peered in his cell, there was nothing left attached to the wall, he did a really good job on it, but he was nowhere to be seen.

Monday, stood outside my cell on social, 10am, a huge thud, followed by the guard's alarm and whistle. Looking over the railings down to the bottom floor was a guy laying face first on the floor. Everyone came out their cells or ran down to get closer to the action.

The man was unconscious, puking and also blood was coming out of his head from the impact of hitting the floor. The guards put him in the recovery position and then ordered to lock everyone away.

He'd had a funny reaction to smoking spice and just collapsed whilst walking back to his cell from social. I started work this afternoon at Radio Wanno and recorded my first piece on the microphone all about me. They were in a temporary portacabin in the Yard with a table and microphone and computer, but I'd hardly call it a recording studio which they had bigged up on their advertisements and posters for the position.

Seemed no one on the course was really interested in doing any recording either and just sat listening to music on the computers for most of the session.

Next morning, we got released for all of 5 minutes before drama unfolded once again. All the guards started running to the showers, the alarms went, whistles blew and we got locked back in our cells. A stabbing in the showers halted our time out the cells today. The day did get broken up by another visit, this time Tess came to visit with the wife. Entering the visit hall, I could see Tess already standing next to the table and she ran over to meet me half way. I picked her up and kissed her a million times.

Even though it had only been a few weeks, she looked so much older. I felt so weak as I held her tight. I didn't want to put her down or let go, she squealed with excitement to see me as we made our way back to the table.

I struggled to keep it together, yet again with stomach in knots, holding back to tears to stay strong for Tess. Hannah was stood up waiting to greet me and we had a family cuddle and sat down, the 3 Musketeers reunited once more, I missed this so so much.

Tess was sat on my lap attentively staring at me and I'd give her more kisses every 30 seconds. My mum was working today so couldn't make it. Me and Hannah sat there the whole session holding hands, having kisses across the table and exchanging words of love and support. Tess would ask me so many questions about why I had to be here, why I wasn't coming back and when I would be coming home. She still didn't realize it was a prison and we shielded her the best we could and making it out as though I was stuck here on work, it broke me.

The hour passed in a flash and guards waved everyone out. We had our final goodbyes, kissed, hugged and watching Tess wave goodbye as she went out of sight made me feel sick to my stomach. I felt so alone.

Back in the cell, high again from the sugar intake from 2 Twirls, Twix and 2 cokes I reminisced about all the things we had talked about, the heartache started to fade as I was so thankful and recharged from seeing them in person.

The following week me and Garrison both got into full time work, me doing the mornings 8-11:30 at Radio Wanno, and Garrison at an IT course, then at 2-4:30pm back at the radio station whilst Garrison worked in the recycling unit.

G Wing was the standard wing for C Cat prisoners, H Wing was for more enhanced prisoners with full time work, you get let out your cell for longer, more access to the gym and treated better. We talked about moving over to H Wing together and Garrison had apparently spoken to the Locations Officer to let us know when there was a spare cell for both of us to move into.

Friday, no one was let out for work, and instead 8:30am came and they let everyone out for exercise. Garrison stayed in bed from arguing all night with his now on/off girlfriend. The phone can be a blessing and a curse. After many laps in the sun, I wandered back to the cell to find Garrison missing which was unusual and the door was unlocked. I went to switch the TV on and there was no power to it. I looked round the back and oddly, the power cable had been snipped and the aerial was missing.

Door opens, in walks Garrison all flustered. I asked if he knew what had happened to the TV. "Yeah, bad news I'm afraid. I'm moving out with Santa on Recycling down to level 1 and it's first in that keeps the gear but don't worry I've spoke to the guard to replace your aerial" Then he went on a verbal rampage about his girlfriend to deviate the conversation from his snidey switcheroo of the TV and thieving of the aerial.

Turns out she had now blocked his number and texts and they were no longer an item as he slid back out the door. He took his bag of goods and left me sat there in silence with no tv, most things removed from the cell and things we had saved together like toilet roll, condiments and equipment such as cleaning items and cutlery, bare minimum was left for me.

I had brought a lot from E Wing with me into our cell, cleaning clothes, spray bottles, cereal, milks and sugars which were also missing. It seems trivial but these things are rare to get hold of in prison and the little things mean a lot. I asked every guard that walked by to try and get a replacement TV lead and aerial, and each said they would get one and come back and no one returned. Eventually I resorted to pressing the room service button, the concierge seemed miffed that my enquiry was just about an aerial, pledged to come back but ,of course, never did. I eventually resorted to twisting the 2 exposed power cables together and plugged it in. I then got 50 paperclips and daisy chained them into a makeshift arial, all I could get was BBC1 but it was better than nothing.

Just before dinner Garrison knocked on the door clinging to an aerial lead and wanted to swap for his shower gel which he left in the cell. The door was opened by the guard for dinner and we made the swap.

As soon as I'd eaten, I was desperate to call Hannah to tell her about the day's events and, the negative part, our lengthy evening phone calls had also gone with Garrison as he took his iphone with him. Quickly, with only 5 mins limit, I told her all about what had happened. I was in a total daze with shock and despair - yet another cell mate. I just wanted to be home and tears formed in my eyes as I looked at the family pictures I'd stuck up on the wall with toothpaste.

To round the day off nicely, just as East Enders started at 8pm, the next-door neighbor to the right decided to have a spice attack. As the guards opened his cell he shouted 'ATTACK ATTACK ATTACK' dived out his cell at the guard who jumped out the way and he ended up going head first into the railings. Whistle, alarms and heavy footfall followed past our cell and shut my flap in the door so I could no longer see the action unfold. I still peered through the gap in the door frame as they carried him like a crab sideways down the stairs. Today also marks 1 month in prison, what a way to round the month off.

Just when I thought life couldn't be more cruel, I had a bunch of paperwork posted through the door. Loads of the applications which I'd made had been returned with a covering letter from OMU (Offender Management Unit).

When I first arrived, I requested a transfer to a prison closer to home whether it be Winchester, Guys Marsh or somewhere like Erlestoke, anywhere closer to the south coast. All requests denied, apparently due to going to Southwark Court, this is my nearest prison. It was a crushing blow. Another application to transfer to a Cat D prison, denied! "Your Remaining sentence needs to be under 2 years to be eligible for Cat D".

The other question which I asked was about HDC which Gary my solicitor had mentioned to me who said I wouldn't serve the whole sentence in prison as I could get a max of 4 and a half months on HDC (Tag).

I ripped open the letter frantically, eager to potentially relay the good news to Hannah. There were 3 boxes on the form, The HDC date - Blank, but the release box had my date which was the full 2 and a half years and the 3rd was the full 5 year sentence date which was passed down by the judge.

My heart stopped, there was a paragraph explaining underneath. 'HDC is only eligible for prisoners with a sentence of less than 4 years. When Garrison moved out, I immediately took prime position on the bottom bunk which I just sat and cried before calling Hannah to relay the awful news, she cried.

We were both absolutely gutted and felt lied to. Clearly, Gary, a law solicitor, didn't know his laws and we were completely holding onto false hope since being sentenced. The 5 mins were up, she was gone.

Now with an actual release date set in stone, it dawned on me the full weight of the prison sentence, it instantly made me feel sick. only 1 month done and we are only the beginning of 2018 and won't be released until the end of 2020, it was incomprehensible.

I eventually fell asleep on the bottom bunk, feeling cut off, isolated, destroyed and knackered mentally from one of the worst days in prison thus far.

I was lucky enough to have the cell to myself for 5 days. In that time I'd received a letter and some saucy photos from the wife. The note said, "Hope you enjoy these, love you". I knew exactly what she meant and I intended to do exactly that. Her letter said "9 photos enclosed", however only 6 photos were received, an officer must have kept 3 for his own stash!

After the normal 8:30pm call which touched upon the gift in the post and how much we were missing each other sexually, conversation started to turn raunchier. After the call I got into bed, turned the light off and with the content of our conversation still playing in my mind I started servicing myself. It felt clinical yet pleasurable and naughty all at the same time whilst clutching a pic of my wife topless and another modelling a black bra, the tv on in the background illuminated the photo.

The next day about noon, the door opened. Here's your new cell mate. In walks Abdul. He was short, Muslim and 35. I introduced myself and immediately noticed he spoke little English, just enough to get by but he was polite enough.

He started to unpack, sharing each item or offering me halves of most of his goods which was kind and the biggest bonus out of a plastic biscuit tin, out comes an iphone 5, my eyes lit up. I'd just spent £6 on phone credit on this week's canteen. Looking at some of my pictures which I'd put on the wall with toothpaste and some with an even stronger mix of tea whiteners and water, he says, "You call wife, my friend" and handed me his phone. Longer evening calls, here I come!

The feeling was short lived, an hour later the door opens, "Pack your stuff mate, we are moving you to H Wing, it may be tonight or in the morning but pack up". It felt bittersweet, goodbye iphone, again!

H Wing would definitely be more suited for me, more settled, it's geared up for workers who then get more time out their cell due to working most of the day. But how annoying, getting acquainted with my 5th cell mate in a month and now onto the 6th! However, I didn't feel as nervous moving as I did previously, I'd kind of got used to the process now.

As I packed, we did the normal initiation, I told him my story but struggled to understand him due to poor English, but he managed to clearly say it was to do with immigration and fraud. The parts I did understand was that he was making false IDs for immigrants to open bank accounts and get jobs with fake IDs, false passports and help getting into the country.

You wouldn't think it by looking at him, but it was no small operation either. £2M had been claimed by prosecutors but they only recovered £680,000. Ironically, it was his iphone which they downloaded all the information from which bit him in the arse. 5 years and 11 months due to pleading Guilty.

As I sat on the bed to give him space to unpack, out comes the prayer mat, and he stood puzzled in the middle of the cell trying to work out the direction to lay out the mat in the middle of the small walkway next to the bed. Abdul makes his way to the sink, and like a contortionist, one by one gets his foot in the sink for a good scrub and clean before putting his flip flips back on and shuffling his way back to the prayer mat. "Sorry, my friend" he says as he takes off the flipflops and stands on the edge of the mat facing the direction of the corner of the wall. Then it all started. "Allah Akbar," waving his arms in the air, then kneeling, bowing on the mat, standing up and repeating the process for about 5 mins. It was definitely a culture shock; he was so confident singing away in his language in a hypnotic fashion.

Being an atheist, it was slightly threatening yet educational at the same time. Afterwards, he stood up, folded up his mat and put on his flipflops and apologised. I said there was no need to apologise and he asked if I was religious. We then got into a full-blown conversation about who created the world, what he was actually asking for in prayer and that, being mid May, he was observing Ramadan.

He was fasting to feel what those less fortunate felt and instead ate late in the evening. Turns out, regardless of our beliefs, cultural differences and his broken English, we got on quite well and had many stories to swap.

8:30pm came, he handed over his iphone without any hesitation unlocking it saying, 'You talk as long as you want, my friend'. The evening count by the guards had been done where they peep through the window in the cell door and count how many are in the cell in case one of us has done a runner and that's usually it for the evening, you don't normally get bothered again.

Not tonight though. I was in full blown conversation with Hannah, 30 mins in on the phone stood just behind the shower curtain and I heard keys rattle outside the door. I immediately hung up and hid his phone behind the toilet and I stood frozen like I was taking a wee. The door opened and I heard him ask Abdul, 'Where's your mate' so I arched backwards and gave a nod as though he was disturbing my flow. "Sorry man, thanks guys", the guard shouted as he shut the door. I nearly crapped myself, let alone pretending to wee! I rang her back, finished my call and after an evening talking about our cases and packing my things into boxes, we went to sleep knowing it was our first and last night together.

In the morning, doors opening, no one came to get me. I had to make my own way to the movements office to speak to the Gov to find out where I was moving to. As normal, he didn't know anything about it. He was flustered with getting other moves done and said to come back in an hour.

I did my normal yard laps, reps on the exercise machines and an hour later was back at his office. He was nowhere to be seen, conveniently. It was a choice of either wait or go back to the cell to be forgotten about. It took another hour of waiting while guard after guard questioned why I wasn't back in my cell. I stood firm! He finally returned, listened to my story and gave me a new cell number, H418.

Back to my old cell, a final goodbye, grabbed my items and I was off. Out of the gate at the top of the landing, left again was H Wing. Being on the same 4th floor made things much easier as I juggled 2 boxes and 2 bags, I'd definitely collected more things along my prison journey.

The guard let me into H418 but it with it being a worker's wing, my new cell mate wasn't in. I sat and waited knowing most come back around 11:30am before making myself at home.

It was a better cell for sure, this had CARPET! Not the thick stuff that would caress your feet and filter through your toes. The kind of industrial stuff you'd find in an office in square cuts, brown and stained, but still, carpet! The cells walls were plastered in photos of kids, kids' drawings and lots of stock of items, it looked as if this guy had been in a while.

The bed was neatly folded back in military precision with fresh crisp clothing piled on top. My guess is this is an older gentleman. I've turned into the prison version of Sherlock Holmes. I'd come to the conclusion the kids were his grandkids, which made me instantly think, older gentleman, great, no chance of a mobile and early nights and early mornings! I waited and waited, he never returned until 5pm, and in comes a white haired, medium built, 69-year-old Alan. You could tell whatever job he had been doing, it was definitely outside as he had a golden bronze tan to go with his HMP overalls.

Alan was friendly enough, but you could tell he was a little gutted to return home to a new cell mate. He had the luxury of his own cell for 2 weeks since the previous had left. He pointed to the shelves and cupboard which he said I could call mine. However, the top bunk was bare, no mattress, bedding or pillow. I pressed for room service and 15 mins later a guard arrived. Good job I wasn't pressing it to say Alan was having a heart attack or he would be buggered!

An hour passed, when the door opened again and in walks a cleaner that the guard had recruited to fulfil my requests. He threw in what was meant to be an adequate mattress. This was more like a yoga mat, the mattress which are normally thin by nature anyway looked like it had been preloved by an elephant!

He threw me a blue pillow, similar to what you'd expect to find on a hospital bed, but it reeked like it had been stuffed with second hand smoke and was as hard as a brick. Finally chucked in some bedding which a homeless person would turn their nose up at. I made my bed of misery and conversation turned to the usual ritual 'Getting to know your cell mate' V6.0

Maybe it was his age, but I felt really sorry for him, 10 years for drug dealing at his age. He pleaded guilty and got it reduced to 7 years and had already served 13 months so still had the same sentence as me remaining.

The story goes, the police followed him and his son-in-law for a year, bugged their phones and cars, 24-hour surveillance and after a huge coke and weed pickup, they got stopped and arrested. His son got 15 years reduced to 10 for a guilty plea only to have another 5 years added for firearms found at his property! His words; 'There was more white stuff than a snowstorm in Antarctica!'

Talking to Alan was hard work as he stuttered as he spoke, taking in deep breaths after every couple of sentences. The temptation to say the words for him was strong but I refrained as I thought it may be rude. This is definitely something I'm going to have to get used to as I initially, and selfishly, found it really irritating.

We set boundaries, Alan likes reading, wasn't really bothered about tv and got up early in the morning which suits me fine. Free reign of the TV! He wasn't kidding, 9pm he was asleep, how did I know? He snored like a foghorn breathing in the whole of H Wing before expelling it with all he had. I could barely hear the tv! It also felt awkward trying to get down from the top bunk to have a drink or wee without waking him, when weeing still felt like I was doing it on my cell mate's head as it was so close!

6am, I woke to the sound of his stream of piss, then flush, then wash hands, then filling up the kettle, before thoughtlessly putting on the news full whack! I felt knackered from not getting the best sleep on my brick pillow, wafer thin gym mat mattress and the sound of him snoring his head off. I tried but failed to get back to sleep.

It was Wednesday, Radio Wanno were in the process of moving from the temporary portacabins to an actual studio in D Wing after spending an eye watering £200k on a refit. I can think of better areas in more need of that cash injection! No work for me until tomorrow.

Alan left at 8:30am and wouldn't be back until 5pm as he worked as a handyman in the prison. The day definitely feels longer without working but I spent the day organising the rest of my things in the cell, cleaning the sink, toilet, washing, writing my book and updating Hannah via letter of my week and the new move.

Alan returned at 4:30, went for a shower then food was called, having to walk 3 flights of raw cast iron stairs to the bottom floor, then one more to the basement to collect food. It was dark and dingy but was lit by the hot food counters with serving hatches, people all in a line up the stairs as we were handed a laminated A4 sheet to give to the server to get a small child's portion of 4 spuds and a flattened, processed and unappetising chicken Kiev freshly imported from China!

Unlike G Wing, the doors were left open until 7pm and we have our own key to keep the door locked or unlocked during S&D's which helped stopping other inmates dipping in and helping themselves. We are in an institute of convicted thieves after all!

After dinner, Alan and I stood on the landing and looked down on everyone on the wing and watched the world go by. People were playing ping pong, going in and out of their mates' cells and going for showers in the basement.

I let on to people as they passed me and Alan trying to gain some form of acceptance and make my new presence on the wing known to those around me. It felt more settled and established on H Wing which in itself was a big upgrade from E wing.

Chapter 10. One Punch Cracked His Head

Just as you get into a false sense of security there's always a kind reminder where you are when an alarm and whistle breaks the silence and the whole wing shifts to the end to get in on the action followed by guards running up from the servery to the centre of the crowds then into the middle of the wings which is a big hexagonal atrium connecting G, K and H Wings together.

As the man laid still on the rock-hard floor, guards tried to surround him to shield him from the other prisoners. People rushed back to the wing to excitedly relay the story of what they saw. He got jumped by some people from a different wing; one punch floored the guy, cracking his head as he hit the deck. All events like this would always be followed by "EVERYONE AWAY, BACK IN YOUR CELLS." I'm sure guards use it as an excuse to sign off early as it's an easier shift when everyone's away.

Next day, another 6am start thanks to Alan and another night of sleep deprivation, thanks to Alan. 8am doors open for Free Flow which the guards love to shout (basically means get yourself to work) but it wasn't long until another fight broke out. An Italian guy across my landing had his international calling pin stolen by his ex-cell mate who had moved to the floor below. £35 had been stolen in call credit. Upon sighting the guy first thing in the morning, elbows and arms started to fly. BANG UP again until they dealt with the culprits. Hour later, opened again for FREEFLOW!

I've been on H Wing for a few days now, no real door banging problems anymore which was a welcomed break, there is much more of a social vibe with people standing in groups during S&Ds (Social and Domestic). Most people have keys to their cells and it feels less threatening on H Wing than the previous 2 wings I've been on so far. However, there is still a huge drug problem and seems to be the issue of most upsets in prison.

This also seems to be the trend of why people find themselves in prison in the first place. People have either been caught stealing to feed a drug habit or dealing drugs and as a result end up in prison.

All the stereotypes of meeting murderers, killers and rapists doesn't seem to be correct; I already know the prison do the best job they can by creating a VP wing which is for vulnerable prisoners such as judges, police officers, child sex offences and rapists so they normally aren't amongst the general prison population anyway. Also bear in mind, the most dangerous prisoners wouldn't be in a Cat C wing anyway.

The showers here are like the G Wing shower but more of them. A saloon style door on the cubicle gives you more privacy too and people generally wait patiently with their netted bags of shower goods.

The other stereotype of not wanting to drop the soap in case someone enters from the rear uninvited is also miles away from reality, luckily, most people are respectful of your privacy and wait their turn to use the shower.

I've now got into a routine with the calls, spending £10 a week from my £23 a week canteen allowance (£15 from private funds and £8 from working) on call credit. I call first thing in the morning before leaving for work and also at 8:30pm, both 5 mins call limit.

The morning call sets up both up for the day, but the evening call usually ends up in tears, still painful not being together and Hannah still struggling without me and having to be 2 parents in one for Tess. Trying to sort out finances, benefits, council tax, housing, working, tax credits and trying to afford to live and being heartbroken at the same time. It's extremely difficult to try and console someone in just 5 minutes before being cut off. Afterwards I just sit on the bed churning and mulling over our conversation, things we said, feelings, hurting and pondering what will be of the future whilst trying to remain positive and optimistic.

I'd switch from, she's going to leave me, find someone else, why would she wait all of them years and suffer to the opposite. She loves me, she's my wife, she's the mother to my child and trying to remember and hold on to all our pledges and confessions of unconditional love forever before I got sentenced.

This process would happen on numerous occasions and many evenings after various calls, sometimes I'd have to call back again to finalise a conversation to affirm a solution and seek reassurance. It's crazy how just small problems or statements can stick with you, play over and over in your mind like a broken record until you next speak. All you have in here is time, lots of it to think and to drive yourself crazy. You can see this process happening to other men too with their relationships and you can see it drives the weaker ones crazy, literally to paranoia.

A week later I'd got myself into a routine which consists of waking up at 7:30am, get dressed, brush teeth, watch news on tv, call the wife. 8am, free flow, 8:30 now at work which is a shitty converted old gym space to house some desks and microphones and a mixing desk. Do course work until 11:30, get escorted back through D Wing back to H. Back in the cell by 12. Get lunch delivered which normally consists of a stale sausage roll, apple, yoghurt and biscoffee biscuits. Write a letter or read post which has been delivered under the door. Eat lunch, wash clothes, watch tv, 2pm door unlocked for free flow again. Work from 2:30 till 4:30. Back to cell by 5. 5:30 doors unlocked and left open till 7. This gives you time to shower, get food, walk in the yard and S&Ds. I normally get food first, shower every other day and then if its nice walk the yard, if not I'll stand on the landing in the middle, looking over the balcony watching the wing go about its business.

By standing in one place, you see the same people go by and as time goes on you get speaking to people which goes from just a nod, to 'alright mate' to then speaking about what's on tv tonight.

I've now got a handful of decent people that I speak to on a daily basis including a guy called Santa (I still don't know why everyone calls him that), RAS (self-labeled due to being a Rastafarian), Eddie (the Italian who kicked off about his international phone credit being used), Lee (Eddie's co-defendant), and Dontay and Ashley who recently moved a few doors down from me and also work at Radio Wanno.

7pm, bang up, wash plates, put tv on, watch tv until 8:30pm which is where I make my calls due to being off-peak to see how Hannah and Tess are which is one of the highlights I look forward to throughout the day. When I dial the numbers, I get so excited, my heart flutters when I hear the first words, even though we limit to 5 minutes to save credit, sometimes I'd call back and we would have a 10-minute call as I just missed speaking to them so much, I'd normally regret it when it comes to the end of the week and I have no credit left!

8:40 till 9 I sit on my bed taking in the call or thinking about comments we made or just feeling pain from the call from going from mentally being with them at home to then the reality of sitting in a prison cell. 9-11pm would consist of finding a film to watch to kill a few hours on Film4. 11-12 get in bed and try get to sleep by 12. The next day do exactly the same all over again.

The only days that are different are the weekends. Sat/Sun no work so doors open about 9am for S&Ds and exercise. If it's bad weather the yard remains closed, so at weekends we are back in the cell by 11am. 11:30 re-opened for hot foot and straight back in. 4pm unlocked again until 6:30pm.

I was with Alan for a couple of weeks until the door opened earlier than normal. "Alan, get your stuff mate, you're off to Highpoint". Alan had applied for a transfer request when he first came to the prison, without any prior warning he had his wish granted.

I got ready for work as he began packing, we shook hands, I wished him all the best and when I returned from work Alan was gone. This time I didn't feel the usual apprehension or worry about another cell mate coming in. Maybe it's down to the fact Alan was my 6th or I'd got used to it being part and parcel of being a prisoner or I just didn't really care about Alan leaving after sleep depriving me for weeks!

I got back and to my joy the cell was still empty. The normal process started of a deep thorough cell clean and taking claim of the prize position, bottom bunk! I only got one night to myself in a single cell making the most of the privacy, a nice relaxing private shit and out comes the wife's provocative pics, a thorough pleasant evening had by all!

The next day, when I came back from work the cell was cluttered with boxes and bags everywhere. In comes cell mate 7, George.

He looked about 25 and by his slang and the way he presented himself I made an educated guess, drug dealer. From the amount of goods he amassed, I also put him down for a prison veteran.

As we started the normal introductions, I struggled to follow his vocabulary as everything seemed to have a replacement word from a different dictionary to mine.

Where I would say 'The guy over there', George would say 'My Man', A joint of cannabis would be 'Zoot', Tobacco would be 'Burn' and each sentence would end with 'You know what I mean' or 'You Get Me'. Another one I learnt was police are no longer police, they are now known as 'Jakes'.

After relaying my story which ended up me being in this god-awful establishment it was time for S&Ds. George had moved over from K Wing and as soon as the doors opened, he was out the traps like a greyhound.

I did my own normal routine, plate in hand fetched dinner from the basement to return to my cell surrounded by 3 big black guys guarding the door, a leg resting on the balcony like a barrier to stop me progressing to the cell.

I could just about see George and one other Muslim guy arguing in my cell. Not wanting to get involved in the drama and obviously the cell bouncers weren't letting me in to the cell anyway, I walked across to my Italian friend, Eddie's cell.

After my food, we all just waited for the cell door to open to see if George would walk out or need to be stretchered out. George did finally emerge in one piece but was fuming and dashed off again in a rage, like he was on a mission.

I started to think to myself, this is the start of something bad for me now, bringing the wolves to the door, courtesy of my new cell mate. I'd gone a couple of months utilising 'Keep your head down' method and was unscathed. Keeping myself to myself and carefully selecting my circle had, so far, been working. It became apparent how quickly that can all change.

It didn't help that my fears were also shared by Eddie and Lee who reiterated their worries for me with evident issues with my new cell mate and witnessing the drama in my cell.

S&Ds ended, George returned looking smug and satisfied. George, despite his youthful looks, was 29 and in for serial mobile phone robberies and stealing Apple Macs from a cancer treatment center.

He started to spill the beans on the circus he brought to the cell. On his move from K Wing to H, it gave people the opportunity in his absence to place blame on him for happenings on K Wing.

Something went missing from a cell in K Wing and immediately the finger was pointed at him which was the reason for the drama at the door. He came back all smug as he had managed to blag his way past the guards, back onto K Wing, and confront each and every one who had been using his name to which no one admitted it was them until everyone agreed and was convinced it couldn't have been and wasn't him that committed the robbery.

George was an easy target to point the finger at and didn't really help himself to be honest. It was only a week ago, Ginge (due to being ginger) and Yas (a Muslim guy) on H wing got robbed. Word had got round Ginge and Yas had a copious amount of weed which they were dealing, a mobile phone and Xbox. 3 guys from K Wing came over and at knife point (long shared of glass) robbed all the contents. Yas was at work, but Ginge was held hostage until they found all the contents. George just happened to be one of the 3 from K Wing, the items were sold on and it wasn't long until everyone knew about the robbery, just no one talked about it or addressed it.

This is why, as soon as something went missing, George was in the frame for the robbery. As George would proudly tell you himself, like he did with the mobile phone robbery, if it was him, he would tell you it was him.

In a strange way, I was relieved that the beef wasn't actually his doing and that he was wrongly accused. Although I felt sorry for Ginge, the way George was so clear cut with it meant I knew exactly what I was dealing with. It was also clear George was able to fight his own battles. I think this place has started to desensitise me, things that would normally horrify me on the outside of prison started to cause me no concern, this isn't normal life though is it, its prison!

Chapter 11. Getting Toilet Roll is Like Finding Rocking Horse Shit

I'm now 2 months in, already feels like 2 years! George has been with me for 2 weeks and I've found myself a routine already. Mon-Friday 8-11 I do morning work where I am completing course work in radio production and producing shows for the in-cell TV's. Between 11-2 me and George do an in-cell workout and have lunch. 2-4 I spend the afternoon at Radio Wanno. 4-5:30 write and read letters if any have been delivered and write more of this book. 5:30-7 S&Ds (shower, food, yard) and towards the last half hour play cards (normally Rumi) with Curtis, Sanjay and Martin.

George has promoted himself now to our in-cell chef. When we get meat with our meals, we save it for bang up (after S&Ds). George came equipped with 2 kettles which he used purely for cooking and had various sandwich bags full of spices.

His speciality was couscous and baked beans (which he opened the tin with nail clippers) then sprinkled with chili flakes and shredded chicken. As disgusting as 'A la kettle' cuisine sounds, its more tasteful than when they serve it up in the servery, more filling than the child's portion they serve, hotter and no more bullet rice! We boil our own in the kettles!

Today my world changed; I've just taken delivery of a new duvet I ordered when I first came into prison using the prison catalogue ordering system (they then buy from Argos). It came complete with a fire-retardant grey cover set. I've also been sleeping with a pillow as soft as a brick and blankets fit for the bin. I also ordered pillows and a bed sheet. Both were missing. That's another application to get a Gov to sign and months waiting for the replacement!

I made the bed and got in that night, I felt as giddy as a child getting in. A slight sense of normality overcame me, that comfort that only a duvet can provide, a slice of luxury in a dark and horrible place was heaven.

However, my body had got used to being so cold at nights and being under thin blankets and even though I slept with clothes on and doubled up the blanket, the 10-tog duvet made me feel as though I was sleeping in an oven!

Spice (the drug) in prison now seems to be out of control. A4 sheets going for £1000 and ID card size pieces going for £200. A guy went blue in front of us on our way to the exercise yard through K Wing. He dropped to the floor, was resuscitated by a guard but died on his way to hospital.

It's horrifying to see firsthand the effects and to know that person later died. Despite their attempts at putting warning leaflets throughout the prison the bare minimum is done to squash the issue. Adverts were put around the prison, adverts on Radio Wanno and propaganda circulated on prison walls but they forget people in here are in for drugs, drug addiction and sentences due to mental health issues; a thousand leaflets are not going to make a dent!

The cracks are smoothed over by cherry picking "Random" people for drugs tests (piss test); however, it somehow always happens to be the people that they know will pass the test with flying colours, never the spice heads!

Just walking down the landing, you can smell the spice and weed pretty much billowing out of every other person's cell, the prison has a real bad problem which is too big for them to get a hold of. Guards walk by the smell and turn a blind eye. I watched the first couple of times, like the drug den would be raided any second, but they walk on by to make their own shift easier.

There was good money to be made from it, too, and makeshift spice labs had popped up on most wings. Somehow the spice mix had got into prison, people were putting it into the spray cleaning bottles, spraying A4 pieces of paper, hanging them round the cell to dry and selling the page or pieces off it for good money!

For a while I would question how certain items like the spice mix, iphones, takeaways, pouches of tobacco and even an ipad was smuggled into prison. Iit's not like you'd be able to fit an ipad up your rectum or passed through visits or thrown over.

The answer would be the actual guards themselves, there is a nice top up of their wage to be had by bringing in cheap items from the outside such as tobacco or older iphones and selling them for vast figures on the inside.

An education tutor from a prison had just been sentenced to 5 years 8 months for smuggling in contraband. A small young female Muslim guard known as Miss Ish who could barely see through our window when she did roll check had recently been missing from the landing. News spread fast that her boyfriend was in Wandsworth, and she had been caught during a random security check on guards coming into work and she was caught with a bundle of phones and tobacco. She's now looking at 5 years. If they pin the spice import on her too, she will also be looking at the guy's spice death on her sentence too.

Why do they risk it? Being a prison guard isn't the best paid job in the world, especially with the amount of shit they have to put up with from people. Being able to buy a small Zanco phone for £30 to sell on for £200 or £10 of tobacco which then fetches up to £200, just do the math. 2 packs of tobacco are a nice £400 top up weekly on your wage.

9 Weeks in, doors unlocked, locksmith at the door. £30,000 was being spent in order to replace every single lock on the wing. During a bundle with a prisoner and guards a few days ago, the prisoner was able to unclip the keys off a guard's chain. Later that day, he was on snapchat unlocking prisoners' doors. As funny as it sounds, the smile got wiped off his face when he realised that for that little stunt an extra 3 years was added to his sentence!

For the past week I have been on a mission to get an enhanced prisoner status earlier than normal. Presently I'm on standard status. This means I get £15 a week to spend on canteen, TV in the cell and 2 x 1 hour visits a month.

Enhanced status gets you 4 x 1-hour visits, £25 a week to spend on canteen/phone, TV and the eligibility to wear your own clothes. I was desperately missing seeing my family. 2 visits a month just wasn't enough. It had been over 2 months and I'd seen Hannah, Tess and my mum 4 times!

Tess was now having to take counselling at school due to my absence and my relationship/marriage was reduced to 2 ten-minute phone calls a day.

I wanted, no, needed to get enhanced to get double the visit allowance. As with everything, the application had to be made, clear rules on who was eligible for enhanced status and you had to be at the prison for at least 3 months! I couldn't wait any longer and had to risk it.

I spent the week waiting for the right guard and the right CM (Custodial Manager) to sign off the paperwork. I then got my tutor, who I got friendly with over the weeks, to counter sign it. Next, I had to bide my time to wait until the right opportunity to see the main Governor of Trinity leave his office, which was rare as he timed his escape when people were banged up so as to not get confronted by hundreds of prisoners with their issues.

The form came with me everywhere until I eventually bumped into him on free flow and I explained in brief the main reason I wanted to be enhanced to due to it affecting my family life. I was actually quite surprised he showed sympathy and said he would use his discretion and get it done.

The days that followed my elation turned to disappointment as I religiously got the SO's (Senior Officers) to check my system which remained "standard status". Mr Sailor, a friendly CM, happened to be on shift tonight so I explained my predicament and that evening I was made enhanced. I felt like I'd won the lottery. I called

Hannah immediately to let her know the good knows. She screamed down the phone, we get to see each other more frequently!

It took a further 2 weeks for me to battle for them to get my clothes from the property department and the horrible prisoner-hater woman who dealt with these enquiries sat at her desk and snatched another follow up app for my clothes and barked "People who complain get put to the bottom of the pile, trust me I know".

I actually got an official response from the prison that my clothes were in her office ready to collect, but even when I showed her the letter, she looked at me disgusted, firstly that I was back, secondly that I went over her head. She snapped "Well that's no bloody use to me as I've already told you, your property isn't here". As I bit my tongue and walked off, she put one final dig in "Next time, before making a complaint, how about you come see me first".

As I walked out, another orderly (prisoner) walked by who I'd spoken to about my clothing situation previously. He said, "Your clothes arrived and are behind her desk". I bloody knew it. He said she's a stickler, stay here ill sneak them out and bring them to you. Lo and behold, he emerged clutching a bulging see-through bag of my clothes I'd packed for prison.

I couldn't get back to the cell quick enough to get out these rags and into my own gear which still smelt of home. Finally, clothes that fit and some home comforts.

I'm 3 months into the sentence. Everyday still feels like groundhog day. I've seen Hannah, Tess and mum a few more times now and it's getting less harder and more enjoyable to see them. It's still tough watching them walking through the doors at the end of the hour with Tess still waving until she's out of sight.

Small things with my cell mate have now started to grate and annoy me. Things like him jumping off the bunk at 5am in the morning, pissing like a river about a foot away from my head and passing wet long dirty farts which would startle me awake, flushing the chain then jumping back up, usually standing on me at the same time as he used the bottom bunk for leverage.

He never washed his hands either, which would really annoy me. Cracks in the compatibility of our personalities have also begun to show. If I say something is black, he would have to say its white. An example; I'd say, "Its hotter in here than yesterday", George would answer "Nah man, yesterday was way hotter". Another; "I think they are doing hot food this morning rather than afternoon", George would of course have to go the opposite. "Nah man they only do that on weekends and bank holidays". What a surprise when they opened us up and guess what, HOT FOOD! It sounds petty but it happened every time I opened my mouth or tried to make general conversation. In the end I'd predict the response and kick myself every time I made conversation.

It was also hard keeping up with his mood swings depending on how his relationship on the outside was going or if he could get hold of his drugs. He was so messy, constantly smoking weed and because most of his dishes consisted of baked beans, made no attempt to hide or mask his trumpet noises that came out his arse constantly, and the smell!

I've come to terms with the fact that he doesn't know the meaning of consideration, if I'm on the in-cell phone which is right next to the tv, I'd turn it down before I start the conversation. By the end of the call it had slowly but surely crept back up with George increasing the volume throughout the call to the point, at the end of the call, was struggling to hear what was being said.

I've never known someone to use so much toilet roll as George, he must use a roll a day! I get it that the 3 tins of beans play havoc with your bowels, but I hear him unravelling a football pitch in length of bog roll per session and toilet roll in here is like rocking horse shit to get hold of. I had to queue at the governor's office and demand they open the stores to get me one as they hadn't given them out for a while. He gave me a death stare and whispered, don't shout it out as everyone will want one. This place is a joke! At least we had found a process to give ourselves some dignity, stringing a spare orange dog blanket from the bunk across to the cupboard on the other wall when using the toilet. It didn't mask the stench though!

Using that much toilet roll, it was inevitable that a blockage was imminent. I heard George over the blanket shout "Oh oh oh it's going to overflow" and he laughed embarrassingly; the next sound to be heard was the toilet overflowing and flooding the floor with the contents of the toilet sailing by.

The lovely carpet that I'd cherished, now soaked in piss and feaces! Oh well, I thought to myself, his problem, he's the one that's going to have to clear it up. He grabbed a pair of gym shorts and stood on them to soak up, fuck all! The door opened for S&Ds, he thew the shorts in a bag and into the bin and ran out for exercise. I spent the next hour spraying the place with disinfectant and soaking up his problem trying to ensure that evening as I lay there sleeping and the cell heated up I wouldn't be smelling his overflowed toilet aroma!

Chapter 12. Pigeon Shit, Mice and Rats

This month also saw an impromptu lockdown thanks to an idiot who thought it be a great idea to climb to the top of the atrium connecting the wings and refuse to come down. As he sat at the top of the metal netting everyone had to be away until he came down. He was chanting away the whole evening whilst other cell mates shouted 'JUMP' getting fed up with his noise in the early hours and to put an end to the lockdown.

In the morning we were opened for free flow, people rushed to the scene of the crime and were astonished to find empty pizza boxes scattered around the floor which they used to coax him down. Loads of people have said that after a few months you get into a routine and things get easier, 3 months in and it still hadn't for me. It was getting harder. Hearing from poor Hannah and how much her and Tess are struggling financially and emotionally without me was awful.

My wife still cried down the phone missing me, hurting for me and heartbroken and Tess asking more and more questions about where I am and why aren't I coming home. The family part is definitely the hardest part of prison, the feelings of love, loneliness and longings just get stronger as the days roll on. As I go to sleep, I have a sicky feeling in my stomach, in my head are moments we've spent together as a family and as I drift off I picture my wife and child in bed, in our house, alone without me. When I wake its the first thought, their routine, Hannah getting Tess ready for school, I'd normally call and try catch them both before they set off, it's still so raw to hear their voice and getting on with their lives without me physically in it.

The prison has had a technological overhaul with food orders and all applications now going on to Kiosks which are little touch screens placed at the end of every landing. Great in principle, but when you have people now hogging the kiosks to write lengthy applications for a variety of things from job positions, enquiring about property, ordering newspapers to be delivered to what money have they got left in their prison account. Trying to get one that's available becomes a game in itself. It became an item to cure people's boredom as they regularly checked for updates from applications or debated at length, what they wanted for dinner each day for the week with 2 meal choices a day!

One bonus the kiosk brought along was no more lost applications and the admin staff have been tasked with providing a quicker response to prisoners. Goodbye to applications getting filled out, signed off by a governor then get lost in the Bermuda Triangle never to be seen again. The kiosk is becoming a bit of an addiction for people making silly requests and constantly checking to see if they have got a response, guess there's not really much else to do and it's the closest thing to seeing if you've got a response from a text message.

The prison has started to get noticeably filthier as time goes on. The landing bins overflowing with multiple bin bags surrounding the actual bin itself, people just add to it, walk over it or avoid it as the smell is potent. The landings which are closest to the big Victorian window at the end are peppered in bird shit where the pigeons are getting in through the missing glass and making themselves home in the steel beam rafters. It is pretty funny watching people holding onto the rails making their way to the upper landings and the instant disgust as they realise they've just smeared a wet fresh one on the railing.

The feathers are also a pest, my cell is on the top landing, second from the big end window and feathers are constantly coming under the cell door. The outside of the prison is even worse. The yard is littered with empty packs of noodles, crisp bags, cans, half eaten yoghurt pots, rotten fruit and biscuit wrappers. The litter a combination of people just throwing it on the floor whilst they are walking round, but the majority is from people just throwing it outside of their cell window instead of having to dispose of it in the bins then having to take their bins out. The trenches which surround the building are clogged with about 5ft of trash.

It's got that bad that people are refusing to bang up on the 1st floor (basement) as it's now attracted quite a few rodents. Daily stories from prisoners waking up even on the 2nd floor now to a little fury friend in their cell. People have stopped sleeping with the lights off now in fear of being visited by Micky Mouse or Roland the Rat!

Hearing stories of people's crimes and sentences is getting harder and harder to bear. An example, a bloke beat up his partner in a steroid-induced attack outside a night club, all captured on CCTV. Injuries include a broken eye socket, cheek bone and broken jaw. The partner was beaten that badly that he lay there unconscious on the floor and urinated himself in front of all the bystanders. His partner, due to fear, didn't press charges but the police/CPS did. He only got 18 months.

This means he will serve half his sentence and get 4 and a half months of that on tag as the sentence is under 4 years. In total, for that horrific crime he will serve less than 6 months in prison. Due to mine being over 4 years, I will serve 4 and a half months more due to not being eligible for Tag/HDC. The sentences and crimes I hear of just seem unfair and really disproportionate. All depending on the court, judge and how they are feeling on the day!

It is weird to think of the risk factor; within 6 months he will be back out with the general public, whereas I've still got another 2 years 3 months left in total which still feels incomprehensible.

Towards the end of my case POCA (also known as confiscation/The Proceeds of Crime Act) was mentioned but not really explained. I was reassured, because I didn't have anything as they already seized all my obtainable assets, that it would be straightforward and nothing to worry about.

Curtis and Martin, a couple of my friends who I play cards with ,also had the Southwark experience and funnily enough, same judge and also in for fraud-related charges. They have just received their paperwork for finalising their POCA.

They seemed extremely concerned about POCA and expressed how stressed and worried it had made them. The way POCA works is, if they feel you have hidden assets like cash which you've disposed of or hidden or physical assets which have disappeared, it's up to you to prove otherwise, not the other way round. POCA does not have to prove the accusation.

Their paperwork gave a breakdown of the extra sentences that would be imposed based on the amounts which they think are missing. £10,000 or less would be another sentence of 6 months. £10,000 to £500,000 up to 5 years. £500,000 to £1Million up to 7 years and more than a Million, up to 14 years.

This had never been discussed with me previously or the proposed sentences should they accuse me of hiding assets. Why was I worried? Firstly, because Curtis and Martin looked so relieved to finally have theirs in writing, it made me concerned that my own was still up in the air. Secondly, I'd just met someone who was serving a second sentence of one year due to a £30,000 POCA. Thirdly, even though I know they have had everything I owned and bled me dry, with the way that the investigating officer had handled everything else, what if they now focus on payments, what I spent, wages, expenses and now try and say that they deem me attempting to hide assets? I knew I'd done nothing wrong, but with my hands tied in here and the onus on me having to prove otherwise, it made me start to worry!

I called and discussed my concerns with Hannah, and she too started to worry about extra sentences being added. A worry that played on my mind for weeks. My POCA was scheduled for a court hearing (which I didn't have to attend) in December 2018. Gary was hopeful, however, that he would be able to get it completed sooner due to it being straightforward and having no other assets than those they seized on the day of the raid all of them years ago!

My wife and I both lost sleep over it due to the anxiety and stress it caused. My wife finally received a text from Gary mid july stating that the financial officer had concluded his investigations. In the background they had liaised with HMRC to get my tax returns and my bank to produce all historical statements and had now realised the money from the assets.

They agreed that my benefit figure be £250,000 and realizable amount was £100,000. The confiscation amount would be exactly the figure which they had from the sales at the auction house, £100,000. This meant I was not, luckily, required or accused of having any more than what they already have. The relief was overwhelming and was celebrated in our own little way down the phone !

Chapter 13. WOLRD CUP

I'm a huge fan of football and being in prison just happens to coincide with World Cup 2018. I've tried to watch every game which has made the past month fly by. If an England game is on at the same time as S&Ds, the wing would be empty as people were glued to their TVs watching the match.

If you weren't a football fan and wasn't watching the TV, you'd still be able to keep up with the score as the wing went crazy banging their cells doors every time a goal went in. With so many nationalities inside, the doors were constantly taking a beating with different teams scoring goals.

It was bittersweet when England went out in the semifinal. I would have loved to see them win but glad I'd never have to answer that awkward question of where were you when England won the World Cup?

The heat in the cell has become unbearable. The average temperature hitting between 25 to 30 degrees outside. Inside, and being on the 4th floor, it seems much much hotter. The small window is no use and there is only a breeze when the cell door is open which is not often.

Nights are harder, sticking to the bed sheets, and the heat is making it difficult to sleep, especially with 2 bodies adding to the heat. They have stopped issuing fans to cope with the heat, as previously people have used the fan motors for tattooing. Handheld fans have appeared on the canteen. I got mugged off as I bought one and the batteries and when I got it, it was about as powerful as a mouse fart! You can literally taste the heat in the air when you take a breath.

A couple of weeks later marked a monumental day for 2 reasons. The first was the POCA hearing, the second was my first 'Family Day' at the prison. The boring part first; at court, POCA was agreed that the figure would be the amount items were sold for at auction, PEANUTS, the second, that I had, forever, £150,000 outstanding.

I wasn't going to let it affect the day, because secondly, today was also my first family day. They had completely transformed the astro-football pitch into a garden fete, similar to that you'd find at a church or school.

Bunting, gazebos, a BBQ and a variety of games for the children. Footballs, ball pit, basketball, frisby's, bowling and they were still filling up waterbombs when we were escorted to our designated tables to wait for the families to arrive.

It was such a hot day; you couldn't have asked for a more glorious day and prison had even catered for the heat. On tables at the end was a variety of different SPF factor sun creams, sunhats, and next to it a fridge stocked full of bottled water.

Even the officers made an effort by coming in their own clothes to make it as normal as possible for the kids, apart from catching glimpses of the old grim menacing looking Victorian building in the background; for a second it didn't feel like prison, you could have been anywhere!

The families were led onto the pitch by a guard and all the children ran to their dads with the mums close behind. It was like a scene at an airport with people running left right and centre to their loved ones.

As Tess ran, I scooped her up, showered her in kisses and twirled her around. Hannah soon joined us for a family hug and I was in pure heaven. Tess went off like a shot to the ball pit before any other kids had even clapped eyes on it.

In the natural way that we did before prison, my hand slotted into Hannah's, and we walked round the pitch fingers entwined, we felt free for a second, no table to separate us, no guards breathing down our necks or watching our every move like they did in the visits hall.

We would just stop walking and stare into each other's eyes or make a loving comment, because we finally could. That feeling can't be replicated and as the sun was beating down on us, being able to play with Tess and walking round as a family, the first time in a while I was happy, I felt normal, I felt like we did when we used to go to a part whilst watching Tess try and impress me with her handstands.

The guards had a speaker system which played music and also had a microphone connected. They would arrange games such as an egg and spoon race, 3-legged race and a sack race. Then the water games started. Tess had great pleasure nominating me to sit at one end of the pitch with other dads as the children tried to fill a jug positioned on our heads with water from the other end.

The first few goes, the children actually tried to get water in the jug, it didn't take long before they realised it be more fun to get the water on the dads instead of in the jugs, much to the amusement of the children and mothers!

It all started at 10am and was scheduled to go on until 2pm. Lunch time came and the food was laid out. Pizza's, chicken legs, wings, salad, burgers and nuggets, there was enough food to feed an army.

If only the prison food was normally this good; they should have served the families the normal slop they serve to give them a taste of what eating here on a daily basis is really like! Although a little sadistic!

After lunch the families were free to roam and Tess had made a friend and was happy to play in the ball pit which gave me and Hannah some alone time in the gazebo, it was just us as the other families were doing activities or playing with their children in the sun.

I spent the rest of the day bowling, playing goal keeper with Tess and throwing frisbee to each other, they even let the day run over to 3pm which was a surprise. The mood soon changed when they announced on the microphone that the family day was over.

Tears rolled from Hannah's eyes as reality smacked us in the face that she would now be leaving without me. I'm off back to my cell like a caged animal and she's going to an empty house with Tess asking a million questions why I'm not home.

It was a prolonged and upsetting goodbye as we waited for clearance from security before they could get escorted back out of the prison. Prisoners waving their families off, with the majority crying was like a scene out of a war movie as they waved loved ones off.

Once they were out of sight it was a sombre atmosphere as all the dads sat back on their designated tables coming to terms with the deflated feelings, crash back to reality and realisation that their families were here one second, gone the next.

Back to the cell and "I'm moving," said George. I felt instant relief as I'd had enough of him to last a lifetime at this point. His attitude, cleanliness, habits, argumentative ways and awful nature had taken its toll. I had pre-planned this eventuality; I knew Curtis was fed up with his cell mate, Pete, and I also knew another guy called Barry from Radio Wanno who was currently stuck on G Wing. I'd just left Radio Wanno due to boredom and started a cisco computer course but knew where Barry's cell was.

On my way to work the next day I visited Curtis's cell, planted the seed and I also bumped into Barry on free flow (free flow is the process of getting from your cell to your workplace) and gave him second in line which he was extremely pleased with.

When I got back from work, George was gone with the normal favorable divide of shared cell possessions in his favour, but not as bad as Garrison. The update from Curtis was that he feared repercussions from Pete, who was unstable, should he move into my cell so declined respectfully. The timing was perfect as Barry Hampton appeared at my door to see if the move was going ahead. I told him about the news on Curtis and he jumped for joy and rushed off to pack up his cell.

Barry, a 51-year-old (but looks in his 40s) was an astute, well educated and higher class man and would be a welcome change to the London gangster wannabe who had just vacated my cell.

Barry was in for a £100M fraud, as they say in here, HE GOT A HEAVY BIRD, 8 YEARS! To top it off, it was done by private prosecution by a billionaire tycoon. Barry claims he didn't see a penny of this money and cost him over £5M to defend 3 separate trials as the other 2 were not guilty. The CPS didn't even take on the case stating "there is no evidence", but the billionaire had other ideas!

It took 7 years to get to court, a combined total of 1 year in court and cost the billionaire £50M in fees to get 3 cracks at the whip in court, succeeding on their 3rd and final try. The whole argument was about an investment opportunity that Barry had personally invested £2M in and had returns out of. He then recommended it to the billionaire who invested £100m. The investment company then just went on a spending spree with the money.

An investigation was launched, by which time £14m had already been spent and the bank froze the rest to secure at least £84m of the money. Barry was roped in as part of the conspiracy to defraud and the guy running the investment got 14 years. The prosecutors pitched it to the jury that Barry's £2m investment along with returns was to cover his tracks. Who knows?

He had the pleasure of the same Wandsworth experience, leaving behind a 36-year-old wife and a 2 year-old son who will be 6 by the time Barry gets out. Barry had only been in 2 months and was still quite raw and finding his feet.

He was so relieved to now be residing in H418 rather than staying with his spice-smoking psychotic cell mate. I spent the afternoon helping him get used the regime, where the showers were, how dinner worked and how to get enhanced early to get more visits and his own clothes.

I reassured him that he made the right choice moving from G to H Wing as its less violent and more freedom than G. I immediately ate my own words.

As Barry and I were having a chat on our beds (Barry on top, me on bottom bunk) shouting started in the cell next door, next a huge thud as one jumped off the top bunk, then followed a slapping meat sound, followed by another thud as the chair fell over. Luckily for the guy getting pummeled in the cell next door, a guard happened to be walking directly across the landing.

Whistles went, followed by alarms, heavy officer presence and the guys were dragged out. One to see the nurse and other being wrestled to the floor. The guy was a young traveler, but well built, and I'd had many brief conversations with him as we both peered over the balcony watching the world go by and he seemed pleasant enough so I was quite surprised.

I watched through the door frame and got a glimpse of the guy's face as he made his way to the nurse. His eye was a proper mess, bulging from being smacked in the face and had already started to turn different shades of colour and was bleeding as was his nose. The prisoner cleaner team (BICs) came to mop up the blood out of the cell. What a way for Barry to experience his first night in H Wing.

Next morning, I saw the traveler outside his cell and I asked if he was ok (to break the ice) and what happened (being nosey). He was laying on the top bunk and there was a programme on about fat and muscle. He'd asked his cell mate "What do you think is heavier, muscle or fat ?" and his cell mate, sat on the desk, responded with his answer which was obviously the wrong one. The noise we heard was him jumping off his bed and giving him a right hook, knocking him off the chair. It wasn't just that, by the sounds of it. He had a cell mate a little like George, someone who would argue for the sake of arguing, and that was the straw that broke the camel's back. If I had less patience George would have probably experience the same fate many times over!

The guy returned to the cell from spending the night in hospital, his eye was blue and completely closed. So, what punishment happened to the traveler? When I got back from work it seems his violent actions had helped him jump the queue of transferring to a Cat C and he was out on the first bus to Highpoint this morning!

Time in the cell seemed to go quicker with Barry as we had similar personalities, felt the same injustice from the judicial system and felt the same about prison and those around it.

Finally, someone that was considerate, didn't smoke, had no phone or want to cook every hour. As selfish as it sounds, him having a longer sentence to serve made mine feel less, however I did feel sorry for him.

Barry's was also a high-profile case which gained a lot of press coverage and the billionaire went on a PR campaign after Barry got sentenced, with pictures in front of his dockyard and big freight ships. Now Barry, a previous millionaire himself, stood in his prison clothes spending his prison money on the phone trying to keep his family together and cooing to his 2-year-old son down the phone. Poor Barry!

Chapter 13. Throwing Poo

My computer course got extremely tedious, so I did that in the morning and went back to Radio Wanno for the afternoons with Barry. We made shows together, had a laugh, and I found the afternoons went much quicker than the mornings.

We always had to walk through D Wing to get to and from Radio Wanno with the station being at the end of the wing. D Wing is Drug Wing, everyone is dosed up to their eyeballs on the substitute drug of choice should it be methadone, alcohol substitution, painkillers. You name it, they are supplied it to keep them at bay and quiet.

Walking through is like walking amongst zombies. Jack from D Wing also did the Radio Wanno course; well I say he does the course, he turns up, listens to music and returns to his cell. Today he never showed and we were also late being picked up and returned to H Wing and this was due to an incident on D Wing involving, no other than Jack!

You never get to hear details, just the alarms or whistles until you do some investigating yourself to find out what really went on. When we finally got to walk back through D Wing, it was desolate. It was weirdly clean but had a strong concoction of disinfectant and feaces in the air.

We got as far as the door on the other side of D Wing before being held up again, more alarms, whistles and another incident above us involving a nurse being spat at for not giving out medication.

We didn't see jack for another week. Jack was a normal looking guy and had found out he was placed on basic so reduced funds, visits and a bad mark against his name with no explanation or incident. He was also told this would last 2 weeks! The main officer on the wing had taken a disliking to Jack as soon as she took over D Wing and after Jack's complaint said she would look into it. She returned to say she doesn't know where he got 2 weeks from, its actually 4 on the system; she had gone away to add another 2 weeks due to him complaining. She also told him there was a note on his file saying he had mental health issues and should be assessed, which he claims she added to piss him off. Oh and it definitely worked!

He went mental after she locked his door back up, he pushed his room service button and she kept him locked up for the week, no work, S&Ds or exercise. When they finally opened his door, he spat at guards, flooded the cell twice, and broke the toilet, but none of that holds significance to what he did for the grand finale.

He waited until doors were unlocked, when she was back on duty, and asked other guards to get her to come to his cell as he wanted to apologise and discuss the change in his status on the system. He prepared for her arrival, a knock on the door in only a way a screw does, as she walked in, he confirmed his target, FIRE! He started to throw lumps of shit towards her face. Direct hit! When I say he peppered her, that's an understatement and when I say he prepared himself for her, he covered himself in shit as a defence mechanism so when the inevitable happened and she called for backup, who wants to wrestle a guy covered in their own excrement!

I stood there in awe and asked whether the shit was fresh out the tap or he'd stored the logs like ammo on the side ready for the enemy's arrival. Turned out he had a stock, which me and Barry took great pleasure throughout the day shouting 'Duck' every time we saw Jack, and this is why we were late being picked up that day from Radio Wanno. Thanks Jack!

He must have started a trend. 2 days later we were picked up from Radio Wanno and hurried back into Trinity. In the middle where the wings meet was a brown slop all over the floor which was in the process of being cleaned. We investigated on the way back to our cell and were told no S&Ds tonight due to a serious incident.

We were 30 minutes too late to witness the incident, luckily. Someone in their cell had stored up a week's worth of piss and shit in a bucket. Their target was a female office in her mid-20's who he had an argument with a few weeks back. As she made her way to the office in the centre, he emptied the contents from the 3rd floor which was a direct hit straight onto her head, poor girl!

Bank Holiday brought another lockdown due to another death, this time on C Wing. It's the 3rd I'd actually heard about and I've only been here 4 months, yet again due to a spice attack.

The food is now a no-go, as after each time I have a meat-based meal I seem to have chronic stomach pains. I got speaking to a few more people over time with one who works in the kitchens.

Unfortunately, I had my worst nightmares confirmed. Turkey 3 months out of date and they were instructed to still serve it, the cleanliness of the place is only skin deep and things get reheated from the day before. It always baffled me as to why we were only served the left legs of the chicken imported from China? Finally, the majority of the people that work in the kitchen are from the VP wings which consists of paedophiles and nonces. I've never eaten so much cereal and packets of noodles in my life! Each week now I order tins of beans to heat up in the kettle to keep me going.

5 months through and only a month away from 6 months done, which means under 24 months left. This means I would be finally eligible for Cat D status and get the fuck out of here! I won't hold my breath though as there is a waiting list of 6 months to transfer out to a Cat D prison, the sooner I can get on the list the better.

I'm trying to get to Ford prison which is just down the road from Brighton so will be easier to get to from the South rather than all the way to London each time the family visits. Open prison also means I get day release and overnight resettlement which increases to 5 days and 4 nights at home, pure heaven compared to what I've currently got. 4-hour visitation tokens per month! You also get to apply for paid work at Cat D which will help getting money behind me ready for my eventual release.

The regime has also changed here for the worse. We were getting out twice at the weekends which, due to staff shortages, has been reduced to just one. The evenings have also got shorter and shorter and now rarely do we get more than 6 till 7pm to do everything, get dinner, shower and exercise. If it's a Bank Holiday, staff training or an incident has happened, we are lucky to get even that time out the cell, with 23 hours bang up.

A barrister has somehow found himself as a guest of one the Queen's finest establishments and was disgusted at how inhumanely we were all living. He stood in the middle of the 3 wings in the atrium and refused to bang up and demanded to speak to the Trinity Governor. He did a sit-down protest in front of everyone thinking it would make a difference.

It didn't last long, the officers bent him up, carried him and threw him in his cell. The female officer who had the shit chucked over her was aiding with the physicality of putting him in the cell and getting the door shut. The barrister, not pleased with being manhandled, spat at her in anger, she saw red and started throwing punches at the barrister in the face whilst still being held down by 2 other officers.

For some reason they then took him back out the cell and down the Block (out the way of preying eyes). He claims that he was stripped, held down, spread open his legs and arsehole to 'Check for Drugs'. The female officer was investigated for ABH and the 2 other officers for sexual abuse. The barrister left the prison a week later.

Walking by people's cells, not only do you get a mixture of smells from cooking, tobacco, sweat and weed but also conversations of people on loudspeaker on their mobiles or on Facetime. It seems the only person without a mobile is me, there's more phones in here than Carphone

Warehouse. It would also give PC World a run for its money. I've seen Xbox Ones, ipads, Samsung tablets, streaming sticks which tether to people's mobiles to watch movies or Netflix, sport or sky. People are selling DVD players with a built-in hard drive full of movies and porn for over £1000! If you've got the money to spare, you could live quite comfortably with the amount of contraband you could buy, but it's not cheap!

All control on the wings now seems to be lost. Due to staff cuts, the job roles cut including quite a vital one in my opinion - the Movements Officer.

The Movements Officer had everyone's picture on a card and a board on the wall. If you wanted to move cells, you had to get confirmation from the Movements Officer first. They would then consider the compatibility of the cell mates, types of crime, age, race and religion before authorising the move.

By removing this vital role, you're allowing gang members to be together, violent prisoners with older vulnerable prisoners and the wings are now awash with gangs from the same areas, rapists, killers and people that are definitely not Cat C criteria. Trinity is being used as an overflow from the main prison and it feels like E Wing all over again! The atmosphere is tense to say the least.

Once reserved for workers, H Wing is now no longer and there is now no difference between G, K and H; it's turned into a cesspit of criminality with gang mentality. The SO on the wing which oversees the general prison officers' roles also now doubled up as Movements Officer and would just agree any move to keep the peace, which did the opposite.

"Beef from Road" now escalates quickly, with rival gangs taking base on different wings and often fight in no-man's land in the middle atrium. One rival spotted another getting medication and 3 of them jumped him throwing in anything they could land, fists, elbows, legs, knees, feet until the guards broke it up. He was beaten so bad his clothes were torn, he could barely stand and had blood coming out of every orifice. In the bundle and out of sight, they also managed to cut him multiple times with a prison made shank which was a razor blade melted onto the end of a toothbrush. The blood was rushing down his arms and dripping from his fingertips down to the floor.

The guards were clueless, as shocked to see him emerge in the state that he did that the 3 perpetrators slipped off back onto K Wing without being able to be identified by the guards who broke up the attack.

Chapter 14. Get a Prison Suite Upgrade

I never thought that there would be a hierarchy for prisoners to gain more privileges depending on the seriousness or notoriety of their crime. In K Wing at basement level, K1, they have their own servery, kitchen, exercise room, tv room with a 50inch TV and the doors are never locked, only the gates to gain access to K1.

I managed to gain access to K1 whilst delivering Radio Wanno leaflets and I'd never seen someone's cell so kitted out as they had theirs on K1. All cells were single occupancy, most had a PlayStation, Xbox or DVD hard drive box with every movie or series installed.

There was a punch bag at the end of the wing and at the other end, a little room with microwave, toaster and kettle like a staff room for the prisoners. Apart from the lack of natural light and the mice problem to contend with due to being in the basement, it was heaven compared to the shit hole conditions we were living in.

The K1 treatment hadn't gone unnoticed with other prisoners, rumours about K1 being treated as a 'super enhanced' wing got round and apparently the Governor of Trinity personally picked who he would like to reside in K1 which included the Stephen Lawrence killer, a member of the Hatton Garden robbery and some other big time drug dealers serving over 14 years.

The officers justified it calling it a Cat C VP wing, yet they roamed the yard with the rest of us. Maybe if my own crime had been more high profile I'd get treated better and find myself in the 'super enhanced' K1 Wing?

14th September 2018, the working environment, atmosphere and safety had finally become unbearable for the staff to work in. As usual, no communication within the prison, and when 8am came and people were ready to be unlocked for work, no one ever came, no one was to be seen.

We sat and turned on the news and got the information from them as to the reason why the prison had no staff, they had all walked out in protest! The reporter was stood outside of the prison filming the staff refusing to come into work due to violence, fear of safety and working conditions.

Prisoners getting wind that the prison currently had no staff turned into animals, howling at the doors, throwing chairs at their doors and one prisoner thought he'd rub salt into the wound by throwing a bucket of piss over them as they stood outside the prison protesting.

Eventually, after negotiations between the union and government, the protest was deemed unlawful and they returned to their positions after midday.

The protest had no effect whatsoever and conditions over the following weeks got worse. Someone climbed onto the railings above the Meds hatch and refused to come down. Later that afternoon I saw someone climbing up onto the rafters and refusing to bang up. We were all put away but I could see him precariously balanced between 2 pipes touching the roof just outside my cell door. My stomach would go each time I thought he'd lost his balance. 4 hours later, a handful of negotiators and a few rotations of staff, the national team were brought in with a big bouncy castle to get him down.

11pm, just as I was settling down for the evening, the embarrassment for the officers wasn't over. A prisoner has escaped! For 2 weeks me and Barry had been hearing someone annoyingly constantly banging their wall, which wasn't unusual, but people normally choose the door to bang. The banging was actually the sound of him chiseling away at the wall once the final check had been done at night.

This prisoner has got to be given an award for the dumbest escape. He chiseled his way back into the prison, back onto the wing, rather than through the exterior wall! The cell had an old serving hatch which had been bricked up which was around 1 ft wide by 3 ft high. On the other side was a poster on the wing wall which hid his ongoing project.

Eventually he broke through and was able to push the surrounding wall to create a hole big enough to fit through. The prisoner was a serious spice head, which figures why he broke back into the prison. The guards went on a wild goose chase round the wing trying to round him up. It was the most comical thing I'd seen, like a sketch from Benny Hill as he ducked and dived to avoid capture and used the middle netting as a trampoline to make an escape.

He eventually made his way back to his cell and through the wall to evade capture. The guy was put in a yellow and green clown suit (to signify him being an escape risk) and shipped out 3 days later. Subsequent to the escape, 3 officers were tasked to go to each cell and check for contraband, tools and any other holes. Posters and pictures were also banned from being put on the walls. Talk about too little too late.

6 months into my sentence, I've still not been recategorised which is disheartening. Wandsworth has also slipped further into the pits, the prison has changed status to a remand prison which means all the London courts feed into here first. People awaiting sentence, remand or convicted in London will end up at Wandsworth. The wing/prison definitely echoes this change.

More London gangs, moped gangs, phone thieves, acid attackers and knife crimes fill the prison spaces. White people seem to be the minority in Wandsworth and that includes the demographic which makes up the staff here. I'd go as far to say that racism swings the other way in here, I've been on the receiving end of it many a times.

We have new neighbours, a kid who looks about 12 who stabbed another gang member and killed him. His cell mate, another who looks 15, is in for acid attacks. We also have a new member at Radio Wanno called Jay, a right live wire who could switch in an instant.

You can tell just by his face, body language and elocution that he was a wrong-un. His case was wrapping up at court tomorrow which he is in prison on remand for. His barrister has hinted he is looking at a 10-year sentence for waiting outside a posh leisure center and watching victims enter. When they left to go home, he would rob them at knife point. A surveillance team watched as he operated, picking his victims in a wealthy area going to enjoy an evening at restaurants, cinemas and shopping. When they re-emerged, he stole their jewelry, valuables and high end watches such as Rolex, Breitlings and Audemar Piguet. He boasted as he re-told his stories proudly, "I'd get them in a secluded area and with a menacing face I'd say give them me now or I'll stab you and I'd show them a glimpse of the knife in my waistband". He even went as far as to say that sometimes he'd have to get creative for the braver ones and hold it to their jugular!

He had come up with a defence all cockily that he will tell the Judge that the knife was there for intimidation purposes only and it would have never been used. Other inmates were impressed by his bold brash and sickening behavior, but it actually made me feel sick. What if that was me and my family after enjoying a nice night out? As he continued to now demonstrate to the other inmates how he brandished his knife I had to walk off as it's just not impressive and I had to bite my tongue and feel glad that someone like that is off the streets. To him it may be just a watch, they never give a shit about the mental distress they cause their victims. All he was sorry for, in his own words, was getting caught. You can say the same for most in here as there is no rehabilitation going on, mandatory courses people need to take or to show them the repercussions and mental trauma that their crime causes. For most this isn't their first time inside either. This place is definitely getting worse and so are the crimes people are being sentenced for.

6 months gone now, I thought I'd feel more satisfied that a big chunk had been knocked off the time left to serve, but it just feels like another day. People do milestones of sentences as a way of dealing mentally with how much time they have left. Each time you reach a milestone, though, it never feels as satisfying as you thought.

Reality is, that's only 20% of my full sentence done. The past 6 months has been tough, trying to keep my marriage alive without physically being present, a non-existent dad in my daughter's life, battling to try get to a Cat D, and dealing with prison life and the people in it on a daily basis makes me feel like I've already done a year in here. Reality is, I need to do what I've done already 4 times over. Not the achievement I thought it would feel like.

The regime in the prison has now gone to shit. They used to blame a lack of staff for not been opened up on time, no showers, or exercise, but after a recruitment drive, they are now fully staffed.

The official regime states food at 5.15, S&Ds from 5:30 till 7.15pm and exercise should be at least an hour within this time. Reality being, we are lucky if the doors get opened before 6 and they are quick to get everyone away by 7, and it takes at least 15 minutes minimum to queue for food in this time. If you want a shower that's another queue. 7 showers for 150 men on the wing! Then they open the yard for exercise if they can be bothered for a maximum time of 20 minutes. Weekends are even worse as you don't go to work and could see 22 and a half hours banged up.

Chapter 15. Piss Tests are Degrading

Today saw me undergo my first MDT (Mandatory Drug Test). Whist on the lunch time bang up between morning work and afternoon, there was heavy footfall outside our cell, I jumped up off the bunk and ran to the door to see what drama was unfolding. 6 Officers were right outside my door, it always gets your heart going as you never know what they are there for.

Unluckily for our next-door neighbor, they sneaked to his cell and burst in just as he was on his mobile phone. They got double prizes as the cell mate also had his iphone in his pocket as they pulled them both out the cell and down to the Block (place where you're taken when you're naughty and get an internal judgement of punishment or extra days). It must have been a tip-off as I watched on as they removed tobacco, weed and phone chargers from the cell.

30 minutes later, my door bursts open, and even though I knew I'd done nothing wrong, it always makes you feel guilty like they will find something anyway. I thought we were next to get spun (where they turn your room upside down looking for contraband). "MDT MATE", the gov shouted in my direction. MDT is detected through a piss test. His timing couldn't have been worse, as I'd literally just sat down after spying on the circus next door, holding in my wee not to miss anything and once it was all over, went to the toilet before sitting down.

I was led down to the basement where they serve the food, there was a black door that I'd seen everyday when getting food but never knew what was behind it until today.

It was like stepping back in time, a part of the prison that seems to have never been touched or updated in years. It was grim, cold, filthy, damp and had 3 rooms (dungeons) which comprised of 2 holding rooms and one large clearing with a urinal to the right and some kitchen cupboards at the end.

"Are you ready to piss yet?" I responded "Not really", as I'd just been. "Here's a cup, drink as much water as you can and let us know when you're ready to go, no rush you got 4 hours to provide a sample". There was another prisoner that shortly joined me who could barely stand, swaying as he tried to answer questions, let alone able to provide a urine sample.

I'd recognised the guy as he lived directly underneath me and had only just recovered from a huge spice attack the night before where he crawled out his cell whilst everyone was on S&Ds and screamed "HELP ME", which pricked the ears up of the govs who promptly locked him back in his room. No real surprise seeing him here today. Being in this claustrophobic medieval torture chamber seemed too much for him, which brought on the anxiety and stress and he started shouting "I CAN'T DO THIS, TAKE ME BACK" over and over. They marked him down as "failure to provide" and luckily for me took him back.

4 cups of water and an hour later, I shouted "Ready when you are". I was led to the large room with the kitchen cupboards and a urinal to the right-hand side, totally open with no privacy. "Right mate, part of the MDT requires me to ensure that the test hasn't been tampered with, I need you to lift up your t-shirt, hold it under your chin and drop your trousers and boxers to your ankles and do a 360 spin".

Just when you thought you had no dignity left in this place, they find another way to take you to a new low. So, there I am, freezing cold doing a pirouette in the middle of this room for 2 gentlemen, t-shirt under my chin taking small steps to turn around without tripping over my trousers which were round my feet. I was thinking if anyone could see me now with my wedding tackle flopping in the air as I completed my humiliating 360 degrading spin.

"Here, piss in this," as he handed me a small see-through plastic cup. I made my way over to the urinal with the bloke following me like a shadow, talk about stage fright even though I felt I was holding back a river from drinking water like a fish!

All I could produce was a few drips, but I needed to fill at least half of this bloody cup. Eventually I got a stream going and I had the pleasure of handing over a cup of yellow warm liquid to one of the govs. The poor prat then had to distribute it between 2 test tubes, whilst looking like a child with a chemistry set, which he sealed and sent off for testing, with a week for the results. That was the end of my ordeal. A week later, the results came back negative for all substances. Now they know I'm a safe bet for MDTs, I doubt that will be my last visit.

7 Months done now, I'm still battling the OMU department to try and recategorise me to a D Cat prisoner so I can get out this shit hole and to open conditions.

When I originally applied 2 months after coming into prison, they replied that my circumstances aren't 'Exceptional enough' to warrant early recategorisation and I have over 24 months left to serve.

About a month ago, I compiled all medical records of my mother having a thyroid disease, meniere's disease, blood clots, wife having polycystic ovarian syndrome, daughter having counselling at school and being 3 hours away from prison. I handed it to a friendly SO who said she would place it personally on the OMU's desk. I wrote to OMU on the computer to ask if they had an update regarding the paperwork. They denied all knowledge of such paperwork, or the SO who I tasked to put it on their desk, and stated their original decision still stands.

I had to wait until the SO was on duty again before I could confront her which took another 2 weeks. As luck would have it, she turned up at my cell door as she was Barry's case worker and needed to complete his sentence plan. I explained everything and she looked completely confused as though it never happened or that she'd ever even seen me before, let alone had a conversation with me or made any promises to me "Are you 100% sure it was me?". It got quite insulting in the end.

"You're called Gaynor, am I right? You were just about to go on holiday and stated you would put it on OMU's desk before you left, you were on duty as temporary SO for Trinity and were manning the gates, you took the documents from me and said you would put them in your jacket pocket for safe keeping". I was that specific she didn't know what to do or what to say apart from take the defensive. Her face changed. "Ah, Mr Hockey", she said. Finally, the penny has dropped, so I'm not crazy after all! She said she did remember and would locate the whereabouts when she got back to the office, you could see the venom she was spitting as I made her look stupid in front of Barry, which isn't always the best thing to do but I had no choice.

Later in the day, I had a message on the kiosk from OMU. I thought finally they've found it and done it and recategorised me to D Cat, or so I thought. "We need details of your confiscation (which we have asked for) but until we get confirmation, we will NOT be reviewing your recategorisation".

This whole time they've been stringing me along, stating I needed to be under 24 months, needed to be an exception, requesting I provided medical records and now it boils down to confiscation documentation, it's just a big joke to them but the world to me! It filled me with anxiety and anger. I'd seen people apply for theirs and leave for open conditions with outstanding confiscation. If they needed it, why not ask me ? I could have got this from my legal team ages ago. I even enclosed a letter with the bundle of documents about a month ago with a highlighted paragraph stating, "The confiscation has been agreed at £100,000, seeing as the police are in receipt of this amount in their holding account we can consider the confiscation settled". Just complete and utter incompetence and felt like it was done on purpose as SO Gaynor worked in OMU and didn't like the way I confronted her!

The corruption in here is rife; an older fellow, whose review date for his recat was a week away, had formed a bond with the Wing Governor by being his errand boy. He managed to get his D Cat early, even with 100K outstanding confiscation. What was more annoying, the following week he was shipped out to Ford Open Prison, jumping the current waiting list of 6 months! Watching his last interaction with the Wing Governor before he was shipped out made me feel a little sick.

The little old fellow stood by his side and waved him down as if to whisper something in his ear. As he bent down, the old fellow kissed him on the cheek as a thank you for getting him his Cat D and transferred to open conditions. Disgusting. I've heard of other cases paying up to £1000 to the same guy to get early Cat D and jumping the waiting list. Corruption at its best!

I did a scathing letter direct to OMU referring to their own PSI rules and that I felt discriminated against. I stated, I too will be making my own enquiries with the courts about confiscation, which is exactly what I did. Funnily enough, a week later I had the documents that they were still 'waiting' for. I forwarded them straight to OMU. It's bittersweet as it's just more delays and another highlight of their incompetence. What have they been doing this whole time? Nothing!

In 14 days, we have been treated to only 3 days in the yard with every excuse not to bother to open it for us. It's just pure laziness as it only takes a few of them to man and observe exercise.

The best and funniest excuse was "We aren't opening it tonight as it's too dark to go outside". The place is lit by floodlights, it's just laughable. The constant let downs, change in regime, excessive bang ups and being treated and caged like an animal just created a volatile atmosphere, you could sense the electricity in the air.

People become angry and aggressive about how we were being treated and it's all people seemed to talk about. You could hear it in the dinner queue, in the showers, on the wing, and I knew it wouldn't be long before it all boiled over.

Chapter 16. She Went Down Like a Sack of Shit

Curtis and I were playing cards in my cell one evening to get away from the static atmosphere, we made the right choice tonight. Just as we were finishing our Rummy game, loud, aggressive, abusive shouting started to resonate around the wing.

We stepped out onto the landing, as did most other inmates hearing the commotion. Everyone peered over the railings down to the ground floor. It looked like a colosseum as the inmates started yearning for blood, looking over whilst waiting to be entertained with eagerly anticipated scenes of violence which were to follow.

Looking down, it looked like it was already over before it started as he was surrounded by 10 guards with a soundtrack of whistles, alarms going off and every swearword you could think of. The inmate was a stocky black guy who looked agitated as they shouted in his face to calm down, which did the opposite.

Putting the pieces together, scattered around his feet was his dinner and his breakfast pack ripped open and the contents on the floor too. This has got to be something to do with him getting his dinner late as they had normally closed the servery off by now. He gave each and every single one a fair warning to "FUCK OFF" as he politely put it, before 2 of the govs restrained him. Hardy, the female gov that got shat on a few months earlier, joined in with the action, wanting to make a name for herself in front of her peers. She kept trying to take charge of the situation shouting at him and barking orders at the other govs to get him up to his cell.

They precariously got him up the first few steps, but she then had a change of heart and wanted him down to the ground. As they struggled to even turn him round and with them all balanced between a few steps, she started tugging on his arm. It looked confusing to watch let alone for everyone else involved in the commotion, guards were still trying to go up as she was tugging him down and throughout all of it, the guy was just getting more and more agitated.

As the excitement grew from the onlookers, the cheers and jeers resonated as did the guy's warnings to Hardy to STOP yanking and tugging on his arm. He kept repeating "I just want to go back to my cell", but she didn't listen. It was inevitable, the pent-up anger about the regime of the wing, the short time you had to get food, the state of the showers, no exercise, lack of gym and being treated like an animal was, always, going to reach breaking point.

He waited for one more tug on his arm before looking over his left shoulder in her direction, he then leant far right in the opposite directly before lunging his full body weight into a flying headbutt straight into Hardy's face. The place erupted! Prisoners held onto the railings as they watched on, jumping up and down in pure delight, it sounded like an excited zoo!

It made me feel sick to see how low humanity can go as I watched the poor girl, with the full force of his head striking her cheek, totally unaware, go instantly rigid and fall vertically backwards with her head bouncing off the hard polished floor. She slid, due to the power of the blow, across the floor with her legs in the air and glasses flew off in the opposite direction. There was an instant surge as the whole of the prison gravitated towards the action.

2 of the guards helped the dazed and confused Hardy come to and got her back to her feet as the other 8 tried to wrestle him to the ground, but they were no match for him. You've never heard a sound like it as the crowd made "oohs" and "ahhs" like a boxing match as he swatted them to the floor one by one. Notice boards went flying, signs, pool table went over and it took another 6 guards to come over from the main prison to finally restrain the guy with a mass bundle bringing the action to a close.

It was barbaric and disappointing to see the majority of prisoners turn animalistic watching on in enjoyment as a female human being was assaulted. It highlights the type of society I'm being locked up with and the urgent need for me to get out of here and to a lower category prison.

Its like groundhogs day in here. I've got to the stage where everything in here is finally getting to me. Doing the same routine every day, eating the same food every day and the habits and quirks of cell mates finally taking their toll too. The anxiety has started to kick back in, like cabin fever.

Looking up out of the window and seeing the sky, regardless of the weather, I won't be getting out or feeling the sun or rain. The wings have changed yet again' to clear the 6-month backlog of transfers, they have shipped most category C prisoners out to other prisons such as The

Mount or Highpoint or other Category D prisons. They then filled their spaces with people from the main prison. The dynamic has totally changed. It's like E Wing all over again. The constant shouting and door banging has made a return and to top it off a handful seem to have moved over with their own sound systems which you could use at a concert.

If you liked the sound of Rap Music 24/7 then you would be in your element, but all you could feel was the bass to these tracks reverb through the floors and walls even in the early hours of the morning. The anxiety reaches boiling point as I lay in my bed 3am, arm dead, claustrophobic and felt the walls drawing in.

More incidents are happening on a daily basis as more gangs have moved onto the wing. There's never a minute that goes by when something isn't happening when the doors are unlocked. This time someone got cut up with a razor blade in a toothbrush all, for taking someone else's clothes - quite extreme. Another, where a guy was stormed by a gang in his cell with tins of tuna in socks because he had grassed on them that they had a phone in their cell, a big no-no in here! It's taking its toll on my mental health seeing so much violence and brutality, as I keep having premonitions of being stabbed as I walk the yard or wings.

I keep having to reassure myself that I'm not involved in any drama, no debt, no drugs, keep out of it all and not involved with any gangs. Just got to keep up the bravado, head up, hold the posture and go about my own business. I'll be in D Cat soon I kept telling myself.

As much as I'd take Barry over George any day, spending nearly 24/7 with someone in a confined space is going to piss you off at some point. His habits, routines, cleanliness, comments, no privacy and inconsideration does start to get on your nerves.

Prime example, the past 2 weeks he's been dying with a cold (man flu) sneezing over everything in sight, and how I've yet to get it is a miracle! When he uses the phone, he sneezes all over the handset and doesn't even attempt to cover his mouth or move away from the phone, let alone wipe it afterwards. After one conversation with his wife on the phone about how he must have contracted it, he continued to give me the lecture what his wife had told him about how you wash your hands properly. The cheek of it! I'm not the one who doesn't wash my hands after a wee!

Talk about double standards, like making comments when I'm having a shit, every time I fart, he feels the need to make a complimentary 'wahey' noise or would sit purposely at the end of the cell all dramatically holding his nose in his t-shirt and when I've finished makes comments such as "Oh, mate, that one's a right stinker". I'm the one that normally does a number 2 when we are on S&Ds, he is the one that always waits till we are locked up to dump his dinner and has woken me up many of mornings shitting one foot away from behind my head, its more the stench than the noise that wakes me up!

I'm sick of battling in the cell, too. If I say "I've got some washing to do tomorrow", the next day he would have handwashed his clothes whilst I was out on S&Ds and filled our makeshift washing lines full of his items. Another example; if I say I need to make a quick call at 8:30pm, he will call his wife at 8:15 and overrun the time without any care in the world. Final example; I would block the sink with tissue, put a can of drink in the sink and weight the cold tap down with a weight to make the drink cold. He wouldn't think twice of washing something in the sink over my drink, no shits given. It's all starting to grate on me!

The worst thing that has started to grate me to my core is his morning ritual. I noticed I kept getting woken up around the same time, 6am every morning. Due to the abundance of sounds inside prison you learn to try and block sounds out, but this was too close to home and kept waking me each day.

One day I had enough and decided to just wake up to find out what the hell was waking me up at 6am daily. The bunk bed above where it's connected to the wall had a peculiar rhythmic ticking sound which was obviously stirring my sleep every morning.

The ticking, like a clock, went on for 10 minutes before I heard a rustling of tissues, I thought the sounds must have woken Barry too and the sound was him wiping his nose. I tried to get back to sleep but Barry jumped down, lifted up the toilet lid, threw the tissues in and then thoroughly washing something in the sink.

In my half-asleep mode, I jumped up to make it known his actions had woke me up, I needed the toilet before trying to get back to sleep. As the urine hit the bowl and heated up the contents of his tissue, it struck my nostrils, and everything fell into place. The contents on the tissue contained Barry's love juice, the smell was unique, immediately identifiable and it all clicked into place.

What was waking me up was Barry's 6am knuckle shuffle. He thought he was being sly, but the vigorous arm/wrist movement was causing the bed fixture against the wall to click underneath, all whilst I've been trying to sleep! No fucks given! His 5-knuckle shuffle had me awake most mornings but I found it too awkward to say anything!

Chapter 17. IM NOW A CAT D PRISONER

Finally, a week later, after handing the confiscation letter to OMU, I got back from work and there was a brown envelope that had been posted under the cell door.

It was confirmation that I had been recategorised to a D Cat prisoner! The relief! The elation, not only to get to move closer to Tess and Hannah, with Ford only being an hour or so away from home, but the elation that my long running battle with OMU is over and I can finally progress to an open category prison!

I called Hannah straight away and we had a little celebration down the phone. It must have been such a relief to her too not having to get up at 4am to hit the road for 5am to ensure that she was here in good time for our 9am visit, then a 3-hour journey home. Not only that but for her piece of mind, she always thought that something would happen to me in here like I'd get stabbed, beaten up or killed.

The downside, my friend Curtis who I'd done most of my Wandsworth journey with, was still waiting for his confirmation of recategorisation. We were hoping to get it at the same time but had only just received some bad news from the Kiosk. They are now messing him around the same way they did with me about confiscation. Poor Curtis now faces the same battle as me and the same delays with OMU. Hopefully he will only be a few weeks behind.

I thought I'd feel more relieved once I got my Cat D, but I now feel unsettled. Not knowing every morning, will it be today I'm told to pack my things as I'm being shipped out. It's strange how you get comfortable with the routine you carve yourself in here to get by. Sometimes, better the devil you know!

I won't miss the continuous bang up, smelling another man's piss and shit as they use the toilet feet from behind my head or being treated like an A Cat prisoner. As much as they try to make Trinity a C Cat prison, there's nothing Cat C about it. They've lost control completely. Trinity is now awash with remand, B Cat prisoners, gangs, and I even got talking to a murderer from Liverpool that had just been sentenced to 18 years and they are on the same wing as C Cat and D Cat prisoners.

As much as it causes me anxiety to start all over again at Ford and be the new kid at school once again, new friend circle, new routine etc., I need to get the hell out of hell.

Being away from the family, especially my wife, Tess, and my mum is what makes this battle to get through the day even tougher. I'm now spending over £20 a week on phone credit alone with the remainder of my money going on basics on the canteen such as drinks, toothpaste, deodorant, ketchup and beans. My family are sending me £100 a month and I get around £10 a week from prison wages. If you can afford to, you can live better inside but only if you can afford it!

Trying to maintain a relationship in prison is tough and its basically reduced to a few measly phone calls and a couple of one hour visits a month. I try to write as many love letters as possible just to get a sense of closeness, but nothing compares to physically being there.

It's extremely hard to hold onto the belief that your own wife still loves you, is going to stick by you throughout this journey and will be faithful to you in your absence. This isn't a reflection on the person you're with, but the mental games prison plays. You see many men struggling with this in prison, can hear the jealousy and anger taking hold in phone calls and the aggressive frustrating venom that is spat down the phone to their partner. Many relationships don't stand the test, unfortunately, and you see many broken men go to pieces from relationships that break down over time.

Hannah is absolutely amazing and has never done anything in our relationship to make me think otherwise, but clearly, we were no longer intimate. I still sometimes dream that I'm still at home in bed, asleep next to my wife, then wake up in this hell hole. It always feels the same, like being hit in the face with a shovel!

I still feel bad and guilt that my wife and child are having to continue life without me. They've done nothing to deserve this life. It's an absolute killer hearing my wife and Tess cry down the phone in the evenings because they miss me so much, it breaks my heart.

Any problems that occur on the outside are also amplified in here. Especially when, apart from giving advice, your hands are tied, there is absolutely nothing you can do about it. One bad phone call in here can ruin our day. It stays with you, eats away and you have all the time in the world to stew on it.

Sometimes, as the months go by, we feel strong and have a mini celebration on the phone for the time done. Other times, the calls are tough as we take it in turns to support one another through this awful time and the daunting prospect of the time left to serve and be apart.

Tess has started crying more and more before be reciting different memories of me and her that she remembers or misses. The questions have also started coming thick and fast from Tess to Hannah. When will daddy be back, why is he away, why can't he come home, where does he sleep, why can't he live here ? It's gut wrenching! If anything, this is the hardest part prison for me, but at the same time it's the driving force that keeps me going.

As each day passes my love and desire grows stronger for my wife and child, which I never thought would be possible. You start appreciating any little thing they did for you, things you took for granted and physically not being able to just hold you wife, a simple hug, a passing kiss or tell her that you love her, this could never get exhausted after this.

Being able to tuck you child in bed, something you take for granted ever night or sometimes find a chore, I'd give anything right now! To be able to peer round the door, see her in bed or to just simply read her a bedtime story before she drifts off.

I'm not there to watch her grow, to see her smile on a park as she plays, all the things you never give a second thought to, but now it's the smallest things that mean the world to me right now being stripped of everything and sat in this stinking cell.

It's mid-November 2018 as I'm writing this and all that's on TV is Christmas adverts. Christmas was such a happy time in our house. Hannah would start Christmas in October if she could!

We would normally spend the month run-up to Christmas watching all the classic films; Home Alone, Elf, Love Actually, and the only music to be heard in our household would be Xmas songs.

Seeing the adverts on TV and hearing the music is just a constant reminder of home. Instead of it feel joyous like it used to, it just fills me with sadness knowing what I'm missing out on. I won't be with my family this Christmas, or the next, or the next!

I always thought as time goes on, it will get easier, but it hasn't. I'll miss Xmas, then New Year's then my wife's birthday in January. I feel lonelier than ever! No wonder the Samaritans ramp up their adverts on the run up to Christmas!

In between thinking of home, missing Tess and missing my wife, I also battle with the injustice of being in here, the wrong I feel that has been done to me and my mind goes on and on about every aspect that could have been done differently. How Jay's defence affected my own trial, why didn't I appeal ? Then I look at success rates which are so low you have no chance anyway. I toy with the way it was investigated, why wasn't the evidence I wanted included, it goes on and on but none of it will change my current circumstance, it's just driving me mad!

24 days left until Christmas, and I'm still in Wandsworth, still waiting for a transfer out. I thought I'd be long gone and in open conditions at Ford for Christmas but no such luck! It's been over a month now since I got my Cat D. I've been told I'm top of the list by OMU to get out of here and the wait is causing extreme anxiety!

I see buses come and go and with each one that comes, I expect to be on it to then face disappointment as someone jumps in front of me for a variety of reasons given by OMU on my frantic messages on the KIOSK; like returns due to court appearances that then need to transfer back to Ford. I'm like a meerkat, every time someone comes near the door I'm expecting its news that I'm off to Ford, but it doesn't seem to come and the wait is killing me.

Tonight, I thought I was going to witness a suicide attempt right outside my cell. I was writing a letter to Hannah when the alarm went off followed by the whistle followed by heavy footfall, you know somethings kicking off.

I jumped off my bed, looked out the small vertical window and saw the prisoner who does the wing's washing running up the stairs at full pelt. It was about 10pm so no one should be out their cells.

On his heels was a number of officers and he just made it outside my cell, jumped up onto the handrails and balanced precariously like a type rope walker, my heart skipped a beat with every wobble as he waved his arms around to maintain balance. The guards just stopped in their tracks not knowing what to do and just backed off towards the top of the stairs.

This isn't the first time it happened right outside my cell, it seems to be a hotspot for suicide attempts or shall we say threats as I'm on the 4th floor, there is no netting between the stairs so it's the only point where, if you wanted to, you could jump all the way down to the bottom floor. The rest of the prison between floors has a metal trampoline-type netting.

"Come any closer and I'll jump headfirst and smash my fucking face open and you'll be scraping me off the floor," he shouted to stop them taking a step closer. He wasn't wrong, it's a long way down!

He had gathered quite a crowd. To the left of my cell were about 8 other officers all pondering what to do as he still stood perched on top of the railing outside my cell which was only about 10cm wide.

The argument was all over him being given a task by one governor which he was getting on with until another governor came along and tried to bang him up and didn't believe his story for being out the cell, so refused to bang up and then went on a suicidal protest. Being a spice head also didn't help with his choices, but here he is like a circus act outside my door. I swear I thought I was going to witness the death of this guy; cold shivers ran down my body and with each sway I'd freeze waiting for him to fall to his doom.

The governors were completely clueless about what to do, they were about as much a spectator as I was. It seemed to last a lifetime but was probably over in about 5 minutes. I was certain, even if he intentionally didn't jump, the way he was swaying he would slip and fall to his death anyway, but luckily a high-ranking CM officer came and called the mob off, which seemed to defuse the situation and he started to talk him down.

Eventually it was agreed it was their mistake, it was the new officer's fault and he wasn't to know he was to remain unlocked. I think they would say anything at this point to get him down. It was another true reflection of the humanity of other prisoners as they just chanted "jump, jump, jump" before he eventually clambered down.

He was clever for a spice head, having a final say. "You try bang me up or send me down the Block, I'll come back here again and do it properly next time, so my death will be on your head". His final words seemed to work, to my surprise, and as if nothing had happened, he was happily on S&Ds the following day. If anyone else had tried that stunt, you'd be down the Block quicker than you could blink, just another highlight of the politics in this place and if you're a 'respected' prisoner!

Chapter 18. A Well Timed Attack

This place has got that filthy, largely due to the wing cleaner going home last month, that people are now continuously getting ill. Curtis has flu, Barry's coming towards the end of his 2nd cold this month and yesterday I had the chronic shits all day. Luckily, I took the day off and Barry was at work which made it more bearable.

The wing is covered in bird shit from the pigeons that come through the cracks in the windows on the wings, feathers litter the place, there's bags of rubbish everywhere, piles of clothes that people just throw out of their cell when they move in, and bits of food all over the landings. It's a cesspit!

Talking about filth, I was on the phone to Hannah when Barry was having a wee; there was no decorum as he let out the world's longest and wettest fart. Out my peripheral vision I saw him go from a standing wee to sitting down, what followed was a gag inducing smell.

Most people would have had diarrhea at some point in their life, so you can sympathise, but try standing 2 feet away from where all the business is happening. Obviously embarrassed, he reached for the orange blanket to hook onto the cupboard to give himself some privacy. His trousers emerged on the desk. I thought "surely not?", but clearly he shat his pants. He had caught my bug, poor

Barry, poor me! It's inhumane for both of us to be in such a confined space and both having to endure the smell of each other's insides!

8 months through and it's another lockdown. Every second Wednesday of the month is like a teacher training for the Govs. For the prisoners that means no work, no showers and no S&Ds. For the past week there had been few S&Ds anyway due to gang fights and they had stopped all wings merging, only allowing one wing into the exercise yard at a time.

Today a different Senior Officer (who was trying to make a name for herself) was running the wings, but she obviously didn't make the briefings as she opened all wings at the same time for exercise. Big mistake.

With no exercise for quite some time, understandably most prisoners had made their way outside; you didn't have much choice, either go on exercise or be locked up again as she didn't want people roaming the wings.

There were so many people in such a short space, a yard of approximately 150ft by 100ft. The atmosphere was so tense you could sense it in the air, but surprisingly, as I walked round gingerly with Curtis, there was no drama.

We got a full 30 minutes of fresh air and it tasted amazing; you've got to be thankful for what you get as most things are just a disappointment in here so you begin to appreciate what you get. They shouted "time" from the door and we started to make our way back in.

Tension finally reached boiling point and from behind was an instant surge which pushed me and Curtis forward, with

Curtis being crushed against the wall. Instinctively we looked behind to see what was unfolding.

A gang of black males finally got their opportunity to attack Stephen Lawrence's killer, Jamie Acort, who had gone, so far, unscathed taking shelter in luxury K1 Wing.

Jamie had been to court this week for sentencing over a £3million drug ring and was sentenced to 9 years. His mug had been all over the press and on TV and it was a hot topic on the wings. Each and every time he was mentioned, the press would never fail to mention his link with the Stephen Lawrence murder. Being couped up in K1, today Jamie took the risk that he probably wishes he hadn't as the gang made their well-timed attack.

As we turned round, we could see a couple of the gang approach an unaware Jamie from behind and swing a right hook which struck a blow to the right-hand side of his face, whilst 2 others tried to rush him into a cell; luckily for Jamie it was locked. He was overpowered and covered his face with his hands as they rained blow after blow viciously. It was shielded from the officers as a crowd concealed the action until finally they realised what was going on, blew their whistles and an officer bravely put his body in the way to stop Jamie's ordeal. The gang slipped into the crowd and made their escape, no one grassed them up and we were all escorted back to the rightful wings and cells.

As for the gang, they earnt their stripes and bragging rights that they finally got their opportunity to get one over on the Stephen Lawrence killer whilst in prison, and they even went on to sell this story to the newspapers.

The incidents are happening everyday now, the wings are out of control. Arguments and confrontations in the shower, on free flow, S&Ds and even in the dinner queue.

Going down to the servery for food, it's become expected now that whatever you order, 50% of the time they will give you the wrong food (especially when its something like burger or chicken day as they keep the best for themselves).

Most people just shut up and put up but not today. This Y/O (Young Offender) had ordered fish fingers and had, clearly, been looking forward to his meal and was not best pleased when he was offered rice as a replacement.

He made a stand and held up the queue and kicked off, and rightly so. People had just got used to it and it was refreshing to see someone finally hold them to task! He vented his frustrations towards the servery workers (everyone knew they held food back till the end to distribute it amongst themselves) but was finally moved on by the officers. Having the last say, the servery workers peered over and shouted, "Its not over mate, we will settle it at your cell later".

After dinner, we sat on our normal bench and started to play cards. Once the workers had finished their shift, still in their chef whites, they made their way to his cell on the 4th floor but exited pretty quickly when he pulled a knife on them.

They regrouped at the bottom of the stairs on the 3rd floor at the end of the landing. Everyone stopped what they were doing as you could see something was about to pop off. 15 minutes later, 2 of the group went back to his cell and said it was all a big misunderstanding and the others wanted to apologise to him for the wrong dinner order.

He followed them down to the 3s where they were all waiting. As soon as he reached them, they all jumped on him. 2 were performing uppercuts to his face as he bent over to protect himself, another started kicking and others hammered his head with closed fists and battered his kidney area.

If you've heard the sound of beating meat or slapping chicken breast, that was the noise that echoed round the wing until the whistle went and the gang dispersed; the stupid officers that were coming onto the wing to help opened the gates to the workers who managed to leave the wing.

It was sickening to watch, and although he pulled a knife on them there's just no humanity in this place. As we watched on as he picked himself off the ground his eyes were all red, black, blue, bleeding, face scuffed and he was shaking like a leaf and holding his ribs and back. The way they beat him relentlessly, if the officers hadn't have come in when they did, it wouldn't surprise me if they killed him for fish fingers. Although shaken he tried to put on a brave face as they escorted him back to his cell and went to get the nurse.

I saw him the next day walking through the wing, and he looked like he had done 12 rounds with Mike Tyson; his whole face black and blue. They spun his cell and found a knife and a phone. He was sent to the block and the servery workers kept their job, disgusting really, there's no justice in here.

Christmas Eve has come around. I can't believe it's Christmas tomorrow, its depressing, the day I've dreaded doing inside prison all year. Hannah has booked an hour visit as that's all she was able to get. However, much I'd try to put her off with it being a 3hr journey either way, she was adamant that she wanted to see me to give me a hug and kiss before Christmas.

She and Tess set off at 5am to be here for the 9am visit. it was so lovely to see them, Tess clung to me like a panda, she looked so beautiful dressed like an elf which she chose to wear for the visit.

My wife looked stunning and seeing her was just what I needed to recharge my batteries to get through the rest of Christmas alone. I took that visit as my Christmas present, she couldn't have got me anything better, even though it was only for an hour.

Tess was so excited for Christmas and reeled off everything that she hoped to get from Santa, but my wife was dreading doing the day alone. We both just said she needed to put on a brave face and get through it the best way that she can to still keep it normal and give Tess the best day possible.

The hour flew by, we had a final hockey tribe hug and she left with a tear in her eye and peeled Tess from my leg. I was escorted back to the cell and the place seemed more miserable than ever with a pathetic attempt to make the place festive. One sorry looking Christmas tree in the middle of the wings in the atrium with most of the baubles now missing.

After the visit, I called just after lunch to ensure they got home safe. Hannah was in tears. As she left the visits hall, she is then escorted to the lockers where they have to lock away their belongings before the visit which comprised of 2 huge sets of lockers in a small room. An orange set on one side and blue set of lockers on the other.

Hannah always used the same locker when she came to visit and leaves her hairband on the locker handle as a habit to make it easier to locate after the visit. Today was no ordinary routine. As she returned, her hairband was on the floor, as she approached the locker with key in hand, she noticed it was already open. She opened the locker with her heart in her mouth to confirm her worst fears. All of her possessions had been stolen. Bag, purse, phone and worst of all, car key had gone, and the locker was completely empty.

She burst into tears, not just for the missing items but being stranded in London on Christmas eve and no way to get home, no money, no phone and no one's contact details.

She reported it immediately to the officer, but she couldn't care less and kept insisting that Hannah must have misplaced them or be looking in the wrong locker.

Some of the other women had heard the commission and saw how useless the officer was being and started defending Hannah and demanded action. In the end the officer called for backup as it started getting heated.

Finally, a senior officer came out and had a master key to open all lockers in an attempt to find my wife's possessions. All the orange ones were opened in turn with no luck, same with the blue ones and it looked hopeless until the bottom row was unlocked. There they were, nestled behind someone else's handbag complete with the phone, key and bag.

Luckily Hannah was the first into the locker room and brought the place to a standstill before anyone had the chance to make off with the stolen property. If that hadn't been the case someone would have quickly entered, grabbed both bags and left before my wife could even realise hers were missing.

Once she had been reunited with the items, they let everyone else get theirs and leave, to Hannah's disgust. No attempt to find out whose locker that was who tried to steal and hide my wife's items behind their own.

Having her items stolen whilst visiting her husband on Christmas Eve, then being trapped in the prison whilst her items were located then getting home just wasn't the day she had on the cards for a Xmas Eve, as if it wasn't hard enough visiting already.

CHAPTER 19. CHRISTMAS IN PRISON

Its Christmas! Got to be honest, I didn't expect to be spending Xmas in Wandsworth. Being totally honest, never thought I'd spend any Christmases in prison full stop, yet here I am! What an awful time to be in prison, all the feelings and thoughts are amplified and heightened.

I woke up Christmas morning feeling the lowest I'd ever felt since being inside. Christmas day, I should be waking up to my child all excited about the day, then saying merry Christmas to my wife in bed before we start our present opening. Then we would be cooking and later on tucking into a gorgeous succulent banquet of amazing and wonderful festive food.

Reality then kicks in; it's 6:30am, I've woken up far too early and realise I've actually been woken up as Barry starts a festive piss behind my head. I waited until at least 8am before calling home. I thought I'd be checking into a happy, joyful and excited household and could at least be part of the fun, even if temporarily.

Instead, the call was subdued. Hannah was finding it hard carrying on the day without me and she always loved Christmas more than anyone. Tess was really down too. I asked what's wrong and Tess, unprompted, said "It's not the same without you, daddy, I'm really missing you." It broke my heart, why is life so cruel! I tried my hardest to stay upbeat for her sake, and with a tear in my eye told her to enjoy the day as much as she could as it's Xmas only one day in the year and we will have the best Christmas next year (hopefully when I get ROTLs from open prison).

I spent the day giving little calls here and there back home to feel part of the day. It's definitely not the same but it's all I could do and I'll take that. I also called my mother quickly, and my sister and her family were round. I said my hellos and happy Xmas's to all but wanted to save credit for the rest of the day, as they only allowed 90 minutes call time in total per day.

I felt crushed lying on my bottom bunk and everything on TV was a constant reminder of how happy you should be at Xmas, all cozy and warm with your family at home round the table, opening presents and being with loved ones.

It felt surreal, like this isn't my life, yet here I am in this body in a cell locked up in prison, alone. They eventually unlocked us at 9am with a begrudging "MERRY CHRISTMAS" like they had been tasked by management to say it to keep spirits up between officer and prisoner, I could see right through it.

"EXERCISE" they shouted straight away, as people were still being unlocked. They were obviously in a rush to get us out, walked and back in our cells asap like a dog so they could crack on with their easy day once we were all banged back up.

I made it to the yard, people who you passed on the wing, who you don't normally speak to, would wish you happy Xmas and shake your hand as I passed them on my way outside, it was quite bizarre but a nice reminder that humanity does exist in the darkest of places.

Outside, not many people made their way to the yard. My friend Curtis had gone to church early with being a Christian, Sanjay, my Indian friend who resided on K Wing was still locked up and Barry went straight down for a shower. I walked alone, and as I walked I could see my own breath in the cold morning air. It did not feel like Christmas at all but I could not get the images of what would be happening at precisely this moment at home with Hannah and Tess, unwrapping presents without me, how I hurt, I wish someone was keeping me company today of all days to take my mind off things.

The only thing that made me smile was knowing Hannah would find the presents that I got for her. These were included in the presents my best friend, Ian, dropped off last night. Ian had wrapped them and marked them from me, as a couple of weeks back I sent Ian a letter with a small shopping list to get on my behalf. Hopefully that will make her day, Ian is such a good friend and it's nice to have someone to rely on whilst inside while your hands are tied.

I didn't stay out long as the thoughts swirling round my head combined with the cold became too much to bear. As I got back to the cell to gather my shower gear, a sound of bag pipes filled the wings, everyone rushed to the center atrium to investigate.

It was one of the new female officers that had brough in the pipes to treat the prisoners on Xmas day. The sound resonated through the wings and at the end of each song the prisoners would roar and cheer and bang on the doors shouting "MORE, MORE". You'd never think people would be so desperate to hear more bagpipes, but it was a total novelty and in the spirit of Christmas it lifted everyone.

Xmas dinner, the choices were field and Forest Vegan Slice, Red Thai Lamb Curry, Haddock & Mozzarella Fish Cake, Vegan Schnitzel, Gammon Steak and finally Chicken Breast with Mushroom Gravy. You got a choice of 1, with a choice of side which was cardamom rice, roast potatoes or sprouts and carrots.

The dessert was either a satsuma or Xmas cake and cream. The queue for the servery was enormous and people had been lingering with their plastic blue bowls and plates near the entrance since the cell doors were opened to ensure they got their fair share.

If you think hospital food was bad and sorry looking, it would look 5 star compared to this. Everything was swimming in a pool of grease with globules of fat with the food floating on top. Most people, including me went for the safest option, chicken and potatoes. The chicken was grey, solid and underneath looking like an alien's backside. The potatoes were undercooked and tasted of washing up liquid and as soon as they touched the plate, they soaked up the slime coming off the chicken.

The Xmas cake and cream turned out to be a mince pie with an offering of semi skimmed UHT milk. I risked a few bites of the chicken before putting safety first and binning the rest, I'd rather not have boxing day shits!

25% of the wing were pissed. You could smell the alcohol as you walked by people's cells. Someone had been smuggling booze into prison so if you'd been lucky enough to have access to it, the alcohol would knock them for six with not having a tolerance to it anymore. Those who didn't have access to the real thing had been brewing good old fashioned prison vodka; hooch from prison apples, marmite from the canteen and sugar. It was so obvious that the officers could smell it but they turned a blind eye due to it being Xmas and also pure laziness to do anything about it.

No wonder people were queuing early, one wing out of the 3 went without their Christmas chicken as they 'Ran Out'. The gangs on the servery had kept trays upon trays of chicken for themselves. Barry had been helping give out the Xmas puddings to prisoners and when he returned, he said 'It's a good job you didn't eat that today, I'm never eating from there again. The rats that circled my feet were around 2ft long from tip to tail and a shit load of cockroaches, the place should be condemned." As if eating your Christmas dinner 2ft from the toilet wasn't bad enough!

The doors were locked by 11:30am and I spent the rest of the day trying to lose myself in any film that was on TV, then a call to home, and repeat until the end of the day, where I had my final call. My wife was crying telling me how hard it had been doing Xmas without me, I then got myself into bed and was happy it was all over. That was an extremely tough day mentally to get through and the agony felt prolonged.

It's New Year's Eve 2018 and it feels terrible. In a way, worse than Christmas. You go month by month ticking them off as you go along all the way to the end of the year, until you finally make it, just to get another fresh one to waste! What a waste of life.

NYE also brings flashbacks of the past ones I've spent with Hannah as we count down the year in together and watch the fireworks in London on the TV. Tonight, we will both be alone wishing we were with each other.

The day has dragged, prison has the strange ability to turn seconds into minutes and hours into days. The more it got to midnight, the more anxiety I felt. Barry, my cellmate, was asleep by 11pm, he couldn't care less. I wanted to call my wife at midnight and knew it would wake him but that's the joy of being banged up together, sometimes you can't help things.

This year was the first we felt Tess was old enough, being 7, that she could stay up and do the countdown to New Year. I had to call just before 12 and at least be a part of that. 11:58 I gave them a surprise call just so we could all be together and counted down the last 10 seconds together and they shouted down the phone 'Happy New Year'. Even though I wasn't physically there, mentally I was and felt part of the celebrations, after putting the phone down I was glad it was all over.

I didn't have to worry about waking Barry up, bang on midnight the whole prison as a tradition banged on their doors and shouted "Happy New Year", I struggled to hear down the phone as the other prisoners went crazy. That poor prison cell door always takes a beating in times of excitement. Goodbye 2018! Thank God, what a shit year!

January 6th, 2019, it's Sunday and another boring weekend done. The courts all start again tomorrow after the festive period which means the buses also start transferring to other prisons. I'm now in my 10th week of waiting to get out of Wandsworth to a Cat D prison. Today was no different than normal, we got opened from 2-4pm, had a shower, walked the yard, played some cards with Curtis and Sanjay then bang up sharpish at 4.

A quick check of the TV guide which my mother posts every week dictates what's the movie of choice for the evening, and tonight it's Bridesmaids. I get settled on bottom bunk, Barry on top bunk as we watch the movie, Barry is normally asleep before the film ends. Tonight though, the film had barely started when we heard keys and footsteps outside our door.

Chapter 20. IM Leaving Wandsworth

The door opened, "Hockey, congratulations you've hit the jackpot, you're off to Ford tomorrow". I was more than elated, it meant the world to me, it did feel like winning the lottery. FINALLY! I couldn't believe it and it was totally unexpected.

I looked at Barry and said, "Can you believe it ?" He looked just as shocked as me, but more of a deer in the headlights about how his prison life would now change, an end of an era for him too. We had spent the best part of 6 months together, worked together and were probably as compatible as he is going to get in prison. He tried to put on a brave face with a 'congrats mate' through gritted teeth.

My excitement soon turned to apprehension. As strange as it sounds you adapt, climatise to your surroundings and in a weird way get comfortable in your own routine to get by. Granted its prison but you find your feet, your friend circle and I've been here for 9 months. All of that is about to change overnight. I go from one of the longest residents on the wing to the new boy in school and new surroundings, make new friends, new job and start a new routine.

However, Wandsworth had become unsafe, poorly run, dirty and disgusting. It was dilapidated more so than when I arrived and totally unfit for purpose and overpopulated. The film went out the window as I had to spend the rest of the evening packing all my worldly goods into clear thick bin bags ready for the morning when they come and get me at 9am to leave.

I hardly slept a wink with a totally mixed bag of emotions keeping me awake. Nerves, excitement, anxious, apprehensive and an overwhelming surreal feeling. 9 months in Wandsworth finally coming to an end.

A new chapter, 21 months left and just about to go to open conditions in Ford. The morning came, doors opened and instead of shouting free flow, the gov said, "Hockey you're off-today, mate". I was elated!

I had 4 bin liners full of clothing, food, drinks and paperwork. It's amazing what you collect over time, and it was far too much for just me to carry to reception. Barry, luckily, offered to skip work this morning and help me load my things on the bus. We sat there with the door open, waiting for the Movements Officer to come and collect me. I sat on my stripped bed, Barry sat on the desk and we had a moment knowing this was the end of our chapter, we reminisced about the laughs we've had to get by, reciting funny events, piss takes, impressions of officers and other prisoners and the loss of our dignity in this place.

Looking round we evaluated how we survived eating, sleeping and shitting together for the past 6 months and even working together and the shows and laughs we had at Radio Wanno. Luckily my time at Wandsworth was done, but I felt sorry for Barry who looked like a deer in the headlights as he still had some time left on his 8-year sentence.

9:30am came, "You Ready?" came a voice as the Moments Officer poked his head round. It was a rite of passage as I made my way down from the 4th floor, people you passed asked "You off mate?" and everyone would try and shake your hand and wish you well. I just managed to bump into Curtis as he made his way on free flow. He was so chuffed to see me progress to open conditions and said how much he will miss me in Wandsworth but shouldn't be too far behind me and will see me at Ford.

Going to Reception we had to pass back through E Wing and back into the first holding cell that I started my Wandsworth journey in. It felt like I'd gone full circle; last time I saw this pen or saw E Wing I was a brand-new prisoner, 9 months later I'm on my way out, luckily!

The confusing part, I'm only a 3rd of the way through my sentence, I'm far from free and although I'm out of here, I'm just about to step onto another sweatbox to go to yet another prison to serve another 21 months! This holding cell currently held the dregs of society, it wreaked of BO, cigarette smell, people with no teeth, chest beating and just awful people to be around, yet these are the releases today back into society. Bizarre. You wouldn't want to meet these people down a dark alley that's for sure! It did make me extremely jealous, though. They'd be free in a matter of minutes yet I've got just under 2 years left until I taste freedom.

The Movements Officer was done and he instructed Barry to go back to Trinity. I went in for a handshake, Barry pulled me in for a manly hug, "Good luck in the future," and with that Barry was gone. "Hockey." I was summoned to the same office that I was sent to when I arrived, and I had the same treatment too. As a parting gift, I was strip searched yet again as they went through all my bags and put everything through an X-ray machine.

Back in the pen, everyone had gone, and it wasn't until 11am when I was ushered onto the Serco van and by 11:30 we were making our way out of the gate. As I looked back through the pink-tinted glass, the front of the medieval looking Victorian building came into view. It was menacing but as we drove away, I gave myself a metaphorical pat on the back. "You did it, you survived that place and came away unscathed".

Attention then started focusing on the big wide world around me as people went about their business. Simple things like people driving their cars, going into shops, going to work, the speed of everything and even the van felt so fast paced, even though it probably wasn't.

I saw families and was overcome with sadness; why can't I just be out there with my own family? I was transfixed by the rolling fields as we made our way out of London and onto the motorway, seeing trees, the sun in the sky, grass, but the feeling soon changed to claustrophobia. My legs were numb due to the lack of room, my knees were rubbing on the plastic wall in front of me and I felt sick from the truck rolling around on its wobbly suspension and being full of weight, and also a touch of nervousness about getting to Ford.

It took 2 hours in total to get to Ford and we arrived at 1:20pm, then made to sit in the roasting van for another 30 minutes before being unlocked and led to Reception. After being checked into, yet another waiting room.

The waiting room had 2 people already in there and they were sat casually on their mobile phones in full view of the officers on Reception, it was such a weird sight. They were waiting to go on a ROTL which means you are allowed your mobile, same if you are going on a work placement. There were lockers in front of the Reception which is where you keep your mobile when you go back into the prison. Such a different world already.

There were a handful of us from Wandsworth in the waiting room to be called up to Reception for them to go through out property. Most things, unlike Wandsworth, made the cut as they wrote everything on a "property card" and handed me back the items to take into Ford with me.

Next, a medical check over with a nurse. All the normal prison questions followed; are you suicidal, any mental health, do you take drugs, self-harm, any medication and finally blood pressure taken.

After we were all done with property and medical, our items were loaded onto a big pull trolly and led to Induction, this is the first chance I got to have a proper look at Ford.

I could vividly smell the freshly cut grass, the air smelt crisp and fresh, I could hear seagulls squawking overhead, rolling lawns lined with trees, bushes and a pathway round the whole outskirt of the prison. Compared to Wandsworth I've landed in prison heaven!

I could see the 'Billets' which I can only describe as old chalets that you would expect to have stayed in if you went back to a 1950s holiday camp. I could see a few prisoners as they made their way to work but without the presence of prison officers it felt odd. Not one officer, no longer the sound of jangling keys, alarms or whistles going off, it was bliss.

The induction was a short video of do's and don'ts of the prison, about the repercussions of absconding and being given bedding (no different to Wandsworth) and an ID card, and it was 4pm by the time we had finished. I was given an actual key to room P208 which was an induction billet and where I'll stay for about a week until they move me on into the general population of Ford and give me a job (I've been told to expect gardening as a first job which is what most get).

The billet was just in front of the induction hut at the back of Ford. inside the billet to the right was a long corridor, in front a small kitchen area that you'd expect to find in an office with a small fridge, sink, microwave and toaster. To the left, toilets with urinals and 3 showers. It was all basic to say the least, like you'd find at the most basic camp site.

Inside the room, it was bare, a metal bed frame along the wall to the left with the same old blue mattress, at the foot of it was a small 15" TV (same as Wandsworth) on a small cupboard and that was all there was in the room.

I just had time to make the bed before an old school style bell sounded to indicate it was dinner time. The Induction Orderly (another prisoner) escorted all 5 of us, Ford Virgins, to a big building across the field but by this time it was dark and I struggled to keep my bearings. When we entered it was like a school canteen but being new and being with the orderly, we skipped the mile long queue and went straight to the front. Unfortunately, with being new, we were only given the default menu choice which was beef stew and rice. It felt so strange eating at a table instead of 2 ft away from the toilet. On pallets at the back there was a stack of loaves of bread that you could just help yourself to and sinks in the corner to wash your plate afterwards.

I wanted to see more of the prison, so once I'd finished I managed to make my way back to the room, dropped my items off (bread, sugar, plastic plate, knife, fork) grabbed a jumper and started to follow the path (everyone walked anticlockwise of course). The place is 1 km in diameter, and as I walked round I could just make someone out 20 feet in front and probably the same behind. It felt like such a novelty not having someone on your heels like on the tiny Wandsworth Yard.

Although I was enjoying the newfound freedom, no officers breathing down my neck, I still missed home and felt extremely lonely as I walked on my own round this vast place. Around the perimeter next to the path was a high green metal fence with metal barb wire on top; it was odd as you could just walk out the front barrier which remained open but I guess it acted as a deterrent and stopped the flow of contraband. Looking past the front barrier was the public road and I could see the cars passing by the prison, the barrier wasn't manned by prison officers, and I could literally see freedom just feet from where I stood. No wonder so many have been tempted and just walked out of an open prison.

I called Hannah and filled her in with the differences between the 2 prisons and how safe and fresh this felt in comparison. She said no wonder the air tastes fresher as I'm just a stone's throw from the beach.

Time for a shower, and to not have to queue was pure bliss! The showers also had a temperate control, whereas Wandsworth had 2 functions (on or off) and you were lucky if the water was hot. To be able to control the heat and the power of the water was amazing. I just stood under it as it massaged my head as I had flashbacks to what I had to endure during my stay at that hell hole. There was no shouting, no more "Yo Gov, no Officer trying to lock me back into the cell or feeling like I was going to be stabbed any moment in an awfully fragile and hostile environment.

Tess was ecstatic at daddy moving to a closer and better 'Workplace' and to be able to visit without having to stay seated for the duration of the visit, we can freely move around the Visit Hall which also has a garden area with benches. Hannah, as did I, struggled to get used to the change, you get used to the routine, knew where you are, where you stand, then it's all change.

The mindset is also hard to get used to, she's at home missing me, yet I'm free to roam the grounds alone but we can't be together. If I'm so low risk and a 'trusted' prisoner, why am I obliged to spend another 21 months in this place? At least its progression but it is frustrating. I can now count down the time left until I can apply for ROTLs (Release On Temporary License) and work which will be in around 6 months, July time.

As I settled into bed for the first night, I could feel every metal slat of the bed frame through the wafer-thin mattress. I grabbed the standard orange dog blanket from my bedding pack and the blue sandpaper HMP towels and padded underneath the mattress as much as I could. I had an awful sleep and woke up multiple times feeling anxious about being here. Although I was in this room alone, I knew I wouldn't have a single for long and would be placed with someone else when they move me on from the induction billet.

All through Wandsworth, I held onto the hope of moving onto bigger and better things at Ford, but now I'm here, apart from ROTLs there's nothing else to hold onto apart from the end, and the finish line seems longer away than ever, 21 months in here left, the time left felt heavy!

Chapter 21. Like a 1950s Holiday Camp

In the morning, I woke up pretty early to ensure I wasn't late for the induction briefing. I shouldn't have worried; the bell sounds at 7:45am to get everyone to their work place. 1 ring meant people were free to get to where they needed to go, 3 rings meant it was roll check and an officer will peer his head round your door to make sure you're still there.

Back to the induction hut, at the back was a small classroom with some school chairs. The Dept Gov came in and gave a speech about what happens if you're caught with drugs and mobiles inside Ford. Next, we were taken on a tour of Ford by the Induction Orderly.

We visited the library which wasn't too unfamiliar from a public library and also had a selection of DVDs and CDs for prisoners to rent. We visited the Medical Centre which resembled a small doctor's waiting room. They had an onsite dentist and mental health practitioners and you made appointments by filling in an application and posting it in their box, with waiting times being so much shorter than Wandsworth which was pleasing to hear.

The gym was well equipped and full of weights and a small cardio section (5 running machines, 5 cycles and 5 cross trainers) and on the side was a community center with ping-pong tables, dart board, pool table and 2 TVs with music channels.

Next to the dinner hall was a Listener suite if you just wanted to speak to a trained prisoner (by the Samaritans) about any issues you had, a prisoner-led council who strived for change for the better in Ford and on the other side of the dinner hall was a fully equipped barbers. After the tour, by 11am, we were free for the rest of the day.

I stood outside the 1950s run-down chalet and just looked up at the sky which I'd only just been able to make out through the small window in our cell for the past 9 months. There was no netting overhead, most of the residents of Ford were at work so it was eerily quiet and no officers to be seen. I almost felt free but still couldn't just walk out the front door. Being in open conditions is liberating yet extremely frustrating and depressing all at the same time. I'd left all my prison friends at Wandsworth, didn't know anyone here and although I was enjoying walking round with the sun on my face, I felt empty, depressed, overwhelmed and extremely alone. With no real routine or regime yet and so much free time, I found it hard to keep myself entertained.

For the past 9 months, Wandsworth had been home. You are herded like cattle, unlocked for work, locked after work, unlocked for food and S&Ds, then locked back up, you knew who to speak to and who not to speak to and weirdly get comfortable with a routine, but now I'm starting from the bottom again.

I kept telling myself I need to give it time, I'm closer for Hannah and Tess and in 6 months' time I'll have a single cell, be granted ROTLs and progress to overnights at home.

There are 2 different versions of ROTLs - RDR (Resettlement Day Release) and ROR (Resettlement

Overnight Release). The maximum you can get is 5 days (4 nights) at home and you are entitled to 2 RDRs or one ROR each month. I cannot wait to progress to 5 days at home, it would mean the world to all of us! I've spoken to a few people who are currently accessing the 5-day ROTLSs as they come towards the end of their sentence and they say it makes a massive difference and it's what you look forward to one month to the next.

12noon, lunch time, back to the school dinner hall, there are 2 queues either side of the hall which is split depending where you live on the prison estate. Today's offering was 2 jacket potatoes and a tin foil tub of beans, it was actually hot and edible. As I walked out, I recognized a small Indian guy called Ross that I used to talk to on H Wing at Wandsworth about 6 months ago before he transferred to the Mount Prison. I was delighted to see a familiar face. He had to go back to work after lunch, but we agreed to meet at dinner time.

When I got back to P208, there was a movement slip under the door, and it read "Have your possessions ready by 2pm tomorrow to pick up your new key". I felt immediately filled with anxiety, who was I going to get next, yet another cell mate to get used to.

After packing I went to the library, they had all the latest newspapers, and all I had to do was hand over my ID card which I picked up on return of the paper. I sat there in a nice comfy chair, sun shining in through the window and I could hear the general public going by the window in their cars and the adjacent road. Is this really as bad as I'm feeling as I'm actually struggling presently being in open conditions, its overwhelming!

4:30pm, 3 bells, roll check. 4:45pm, 1 bell, dinner time, and people actually ran to the clubhouse for dinner to beat the queues. It was funny watching people race each other. Chicken and rice tonight and I spotted Ross on my way in so it was nice to sit with someone whilst I ate dinner.

He invited me back to his room which was on E Wing in the same building as the dinner hall. I was immediately jealous. It was clean, personalised with all his family pictures on the wall, and he was in a single room and it was quiet with no one's music thumping through the walls unlike P billets. He had only been here since November 2018 but managed to skip the single room queue (currently 6 months) due to 'medical reasons'.

This time tomorrow I'll be banged up with yet another cell mate, their habits, snoring, fighting over what to watch on TV and no space, these billet rooms are just big enough to fit 2 beds in!

The rest of the evening we walked round the path inside Ford until our legs fell off which was about 4 laps (approx. 3 miles). Back in my minimalistic bare room, I struggled to get any sleep yet again with the thought of moving tomorrow. The next day, I woke up to a slip under the door to let me know my key was ready to pick up from the induction hut. L202 was due to be my new home, but it's who resided there that filled me with dread, not only the cell mates but the other residents that you needed to share L2 billet with.

No one helped me move, so bag by bag I walked it from one side of the prison to the other to move into my new abode. The place was filthy! I've seen cleaner student digs! Under the sink in the kitchen were 2 cardboard boxes which looked like an unofficial game of rubbish Jenga! The floor was covered in rice and the sides splattered with dried food; it stank. The fridge was brimming with half eaten food and it was that rammed it struggled to keep the items below room temperature.

The 2 microwaves (only 1 worked) were caked in bean juice stains and other food residue. The sink area was stacked with dirty plates and the 2 toasters were covered in breadcrumbs and fag ash where they used it to light cigarettes. The entrance to L2 was covered in mud where people walked through the dirt from working in the gardens all day, where people didn't walk you could see what colour the floor should be.

In the bathroom, the 2 urinals were blocked off with tape and still had a puddle of yellow urine in them, it looked like a crime scene. The 5 sinks to the right of the bathroom were without proper plumbing, the pipes from the sink just dropped into a trough in the floor and the 2 toilets were like public loos, but worse. They were littered with empty loo rolls, fag butts, spit, graffiti and shit stains. Finally, the 2 showers which were sunken shower trays separated by a partition wall and shower curtains for privacy. Sounds great but the curtains were mold ridden, the walls damp, trays an off white and heavily stained and riddled with pubes and empty shower gel bottles. The whole area was littered with dumped clothes, clothes drying, mold spores, hairs and empty toiletries. The mop and bucket provided was used as yet another Jenga style bin with items precariously balanced on top without toppling the whole mountain over.

Onto the room, in front was a bed next to the wall, and to the left another bed against the wall forming an L shape. On the left next to the door against the wall were 2 half-sized wardrobes with the bedside tables next to them. On top of the wardrobes was the TV and a box shelf with 6 compartments. The mattress on the empty bed may as well not have had one, it dipped in the middle so much it looked like a canoe.

My cell mate was still at work and there were no family photos or paperwork left lying around so I couldn't gauge who my new cell mate was. Onto padding my bed out yet again, I even added the prison issue clothing this time! I put away my clothes, swept the floor and gave the place a clean. By the time I'd finished it was lunch time and the lock to the door clicks and in walks Kev. He's a 53 year-old white guy that could talk for England, I mean this guy didn't come up for air. It was a nice relief though as he seemed sensible enough, friendly and chatty. His story; his sister was in care and he was put in charge of the finances. The accusation goes, he transferred a bit to her and the rest to himself. "Don't get too comfortable with me though, mate." I thought was an odd comment before he left for work but he explained he was leaving on Monday, sentence finished, my heart sank once again.

After doing my afternoon Induction session, meeting all departments and heads of the prison, I returned to find the kitchen a hive of action. I thought it would be a good opportunity to introduce myself. It was daunting to walk into a room full of unknowns and as I made my way into the sea of bodies in a small space, I was like a lamb to the slaughter.

The majority were young Asian guys and immediately you could sense they were analysing me. I introduced myself but no one was really hospitable or accommodating and pretty much ignored the newbie infiltrating their domain. I saw a picture of a Lamborghini on a calendar on the wall of the kitchen so made small talk about my passion for cars, some mustered up enough noise to warrant a response but I could tell some were talking behind my back, so I cut my losses and walked back to my room to lick my wounds. At least the ice breaker was done.

I started to write a letter to the wife, but Kev just chewed my ear off about a bad phone call he had with his girlfriend and how much of a gold digger she is and although he has transferred so much money she won't have sex with him. I just want to finish my letter! I even stopped answering and he still carried on talking, get the hint!

As he was in first, he had full control over the remote and what we watched, and I only realised he was asleep about 10pm as the news was on and he stopped talking! I had to get out of bed and manually switch the TV off as I was absolutely knackered from the move.

6am, I woke up to a load of rustling. I thought to myself, I hope I don't have another Barry as a cell mate who like a cheeky tommy tank in the morning, I put my glasses on and sat up. Kev says, "Don't mind me, mate, I'm just off to take a shower before work, got to beat the rush as everyone showers about the same time here." It's 6 o'clock in the fucking morning and I felt that tired like my eyes had dirt In them, and I'd just managed to go back to sleep when I was woken again to the sound of news blasting out on the TV That's it, I'm up you selfish bastard!

Chapter 22. My Bullshit Got Me Promoted

It's been 2 weeks now and I've finished induction and have settled a little more than when I first arrived. Coming from Wandsworth with its enclosed, poor, violent, volatile and inhumane conditions to an open prison is a huge change and it takes some getting used to.

The induction process lasted a full 2 weeks, even though there was no need for it to take that long and getting people into another routine would have really helped with the transition. Kev has now left; I won't miss hearing the nonstop rants about his broken relationship or adding "at the end of the day" to every single sentence! It was a welcome break having the room to myself for a couple of nights before Tony moved in. Tony was a 53 year-old family man, 3 kids and in for contract fraud. He had 18 months to go which was a perfect match for me.

Tony was quiet, fell asleep with the TV on, didn't mind what I watched and was out the cell most of the day. He also didn't want a shower at 6am which was a bonus. I've just received a slip under the cell giving me my first job placement, LBA! (Land Based Activities, GARDENS).

Its Jan 2019 and bloody freezing outside, I'm talking 3 degrees. The first time in the job saw me sat in a chilly barn for 3 hours in the morning doing absolutely nothing. This literally feels like they are giving out jobs just for the sake of it, like a tick box exercise as they are meant to be seen as a 'working' prison. Those that were actually doing something were just planting seeds, sweeping or painting garden gnomes.

By the afternoon session, I'd had enough as I'd rather be busy doing something than sat here doing nothing. I reported to the main Gov of gardens, 'Steve,' to voice my concern about my 'ongoing rib problem', basically the bed had given my sides a right pounding from pretty much sleeping on metal slats. He could see right through my bullshit but could see I was sensible and instead rewarded me with a job in the office as Garden Orderly. Bonus!

It was like a rundown office you would find in a car garage, but I wasn't in the cold anymore. All I had to do in the role was check people in and out of their LBA job, so if a roll check was done we had the right amount of people that should be on site.

3 weeks in and I've finally got into a routine. Just being able to go to a hut each lunchtime if you needed supplies such as toilet roll or toiletries is still a novelty. Also for kit change, just take bedding, towels or clothing and they will swap them for clean items. The food is hot and bigger portions, post isn't really read (only opened to check for illicit items) and you can collect it on time each day from a little post office next to Reception.

The visits are something else; my wife and Tess came to visit last week and there's no more waiting in a stinking holding cell before the visit, no searches going in and no more having to wear smelly vests during the visit. There are no really strict rules about visits like being stuck to your chair or being separated by a table, visits were also 2 hours along, it was amazing!

I was free to walk around, so Tess and I walked together to the coffee shop inside the Visits Hall and bought drinks and snacks. Hannah sat next to me in my arms on the comfy lounge chairs and the officers sat at the end of the hall. I had a cheeky few gropes, snogs and lots of hugs whilst Tess sat making things in the children's area which also had a child minder there to help with the kids; we were in our element. Apparently, Wednesday evening visits are one to avoid with the children as they are dubbed 'Date Night Wednesday' where prisoners come back with smile on their faces!

On each table is a slip, '12 items for £10 or 6 for £5'. You can select items from the coffee shop to take back into the prison with you which are bagged up and then you can pick them up at the end of the visit. That's 6 cokes and 6 bars of chocolate waiting for me after this visit! You're allowed 4 of these 2 hour visits a month, it's not quite a ROTL but it's a start

It's amazing how quickly you forget about Wandsworth, and I've stopped comparing now and am counting down the 12 weeks left until I can get my first ROTL. Walking round in the evenings, all you smell billowing out of each billet is weed, but I don't know why people risk it here as they claim to have a zero tolerance policy.

The place is riddled with mobile phones, too, and they are so much cheaper to buy than Wandsworth due to the competition in supply. With people working outside the prison, ROTLs and the ease of having something thrown over the fence, it's never been easier to get whatever you want in prison. People regularly order deliveries from their phones and have them chucked over the fence, even the delivery drivers have started to get good at wrapping the food in bin liners to keep the contents intact on landing.

They also have a 'Block' here too, a big grey building next to my billet. With the temptation great, it is always full and people are being shipped out daily for a variety of reasons, and piss tests also seem more frequent here.

The only thing that I'd love to change with my current situation is the living conditions. There is no space in the rooms, the walls are paper thin and it's filthy. The officers rarely come to check and only do rounds to do roll check. It's a room for one person, but with 2 people and their belongings shoe-horned in.

At Ford they allow a whole list of items that you're allowed to have in your room ranging from rugs, lamps, DVD players and the worst offender, stereos. It seems to be a competition of who can have the loudest and bassiest stereo, I think my next-door neighbor wins! The majority use a 3.5mm headphone jack to run the TV through the stereo and I can literally feel EastEnders coming through the wall and vibrating with each bass note. Most also keep their door open on the hinges which makes the sound travel and even though I keep ours shut, it does nothing to dampen the sound or bass! It's driving me insane!

These billets are not fit for purpose, and while each should only house 8 maximum, like Wandsworth and due to lack of space, they have doubled everyone up. 16 people fighting for 2 toilets, 2 showers, 2 microwaves and 16 different age ranges, personalities, consideration levels and 15 other people for me to contend with, its grim.

When gang members arrive at Ford, they seem be able to get in the same billet or a billet next door which creates volatile areas to walk around in. It's started to get like Wandsworth again with the fear that something may happen at any time. The smell of weed is on every corner as you walk round as people hang out the fire door smoking their newest stash that's been thrown over the fence.

The current waiting list has gone up to 7 months for people to have to share a room in a billet before being transferred to the main accommodation block and into a single room. I can't wait to have more room than just enough to shimmy past my cell mate's bed and the wardrobes to get to my own. I'm also sick of people knocking on the door asking for things: "Got any snout (tobacco), sugar, sauce, drinks", anything they are missing they go up the hallway from door to door until they get what they are looking for, and I'm sick of inconsiderate arseholes!

The phone situation is worse than Wandsworth! At the end of the hallway and in the porchway entrance to the billet is the communal phone, and there are no phones in the cell. This means you are right in the crossroad of all the action whilst trying to have a call to your loved ones. Kitchen right behind, all rooms to your right, entrance in front and showers/toilets to your left, its mayhem! Trying to hear is a mission and no matter how many times you ask people to just keep the noise down or the door shut, it falls on deaf ears. The whole billet even had a group bundle right behind me whilst I was on the phone and bashing into my legs with no fucks given!

The worst was when a chair was plonked behind me, and initially I thought finally someone is being considerate and the chair was for me. I soon realised what was happening as I heard the hair clippers buzzing away and as I turned around I saw a makeshift barber shop had popped up behind me whilst I was on the phone.

There's an unwritten rule here which is doing my head in. If you are calling in on someone and need to knock on their door like any normal human being would, DONT! Everyone gets funny here about the scratch rule. Instead of knocking, you have to scratch the door, this way everyone knows if it's an officer or a prisoner coming to the door. Why is that so important? Well, most people are either smoking weed or on their phones so when the door gets scratched they don't need to lob everything out the window. It is so annoying though, like having a big rat coming to visit with the constant scratching on each other's doors all the way up the landing. One flaw in this method is that if an officer did come to room search or do an intelligence-led raid, they wouldn't knock and wait to be invited in! Everyone seems to have bought into this methodology though, so when in Rome!

End of the third week at Ford, me and Tony (roommate) had been getting along fine and shared the same hatred and irritability with the billet. We had got into a good routine and as much as we were in a small, confined space, we respected each other's privacy and values. This morning was to be different. I looked out the window like I normally did whilst waiting for the bell to release us for work; however, today was to be no normal day.

I spotted 4 officers coming to our billet and as they passed the window I turned to Tony and said this should be exciting and we speculated which resident of L2 billet was just about to be spun.

There were a hell of a lot of drugs on this billet, I'm sure they were dealing and pretty much every room apart from ours had a mobile, hence why they had no respect for anyone on the communal phone.

It was just a matter of time before one of their doors burst open and I held my breath trying to listen to whose it was going to be.

Our door burst open, my arse went, Tony jumped up off the bed, we were both shell shocked that it was our door, of all doors, that bust open, but I'm sure they had the wrong room. "Smith?" said the officer, my bum stopped puckering and the relief was immense.

They escorted me to the kitchen and locked me in there, while everyone else was ordered to stay in their rooms. Minutes later, Tony was escorted to the Block. He shouted to me, "I don't know what this is all about" as he left the billet. I was unlocked and the officers left. Everyone ran to me from their rooms and asked a thousand questions which I had no answers to as Tony was the last person you'd expect to be taken down the Block

The bell releasing everyone went as soon after Tony had left, and I ran to the Block before I made my way to work and shouted to Tony through the Block window. Tony was still clueless as to why he was in there but confirmed he had been told he is being shipped out, so it must be serious.

With working in the office at the Gardens, I'm also working directly with a lot of officers who head up small teams of prisoners there. I asked them to do some digging for me as I was so intrigued about why Tony of all people was being shipped out. Turns out Tony was heavily into drugs and failed his last drug test from his previous prison and the results had just come in. I would have never have guessed, so it turns out Tony is a bit of a dark horse after all! Great, onto my 3rd roommate in 3 weeks!

Me and Ross walked round that evening and had a premonition that upon my return to the room, someone would have already moved in, and we were right. Getting back to the room someone's items were piled high and it makes your heart sink as it's like starting all over again. Getting to know someone, routine, habits etc. I scoured his items; mouthwash, comic books, mechanic workbook... this had to be someone youngish.

8:30pm, Roll check, and just as the officer came on the billet and shouted "Roll check", in runs James. A 26-year-old beanie hat wearing, goatee'd, vaping, immature new roommate. Lovely, just what I needed. You could instantly feel the difference in ages between us and also the difference between cool and calm Tony and hyperactive, everything has to be a joke, James.

The initiation game started and I told a shortened version of mine, while his changed versions so many times it was hard to keep up. Something about GBH, bottling someone in a pub then breaking a guy's cheek, eye socket nose and jaw. He didn't look capable of such damage; he was only about 8 stone wet through!

The conversation got onto looking forward to ROTLs to which he responded his would be escorted as he was MAPPA (Multi-Agency Public Protection Arrangements) so is deemed as a serious risk and would need to be escorted for a few day trips first. Probably not the best start to introductions or a roommate you'd want.

After roll check, another 2 officers turned up at the door and I'm beginning to think this room is cursed! "James, come with us." Thank God it wasn't for me. My room was then flooded with all the concerned L2 residents again being all nosey wondering what was happening, but I must have sounded as clueless as this morning or part of the conspiracy as I didn't have any answers for them.

James returned an hour later, deflated, but he clearly wanted to pick my brains over the topic. "I've been put on an ACCT, and they say you're a good match for me". An ACCT (Assessment, Care in **Custody** and Teamwork) is also seen as 'suicide watch' in prison. They had been monitoring his letters and calls and he had threatened to kill himself to his mum and girlfriend in various phone calls he had made from the Ford phones.

So now, not only do I have a violent, volatile, Jekyll and Hyde character in with me, I might wake up or return to someone who's decided to take their own life in my room. He already had a long list of unsuccessful roommate matches so they looked through, found my profile and thought I'd be a good choice and in effect, let me do their job for them, put me on suicide watch over James because I'm 'sensible' and have a clean prison record.

Chapter 23. Stabbed in the Neck

The billets should be condemned, they really are not fit for purpose. The power supply trips out, water is constantly going off, heating is touch and go (and its freezing when it does go off) and should there be a fire (again) it could be catastrophic. To top it off, the HMP establishment always claim that 'family ties reduce reoffending,' but then the phone call costs are more extortionate here than Wandsworth. I'm spending over £15 a week on phone calls which gets me a few hours a day on the phone, its daylight robbery and the charges should be a crime in itself. I've brought it up at the prison council and apparently they are contracted with BT so the charges can't be changed; no wonder so many people get mobiles, it's so tempting!

We were always made to believe through our prison journey thus far, and after all the hoops you have to jump through, that you had to be a low-risk prisoner with a clean record to get to an open, Cat D, prison. Definitely nothing violent, threatening or a risk to public, which makes sense seing as the prisoner could be mingling with the general public once they've reached their FLED (Facility Licence Eligibility Date) and can access ROTLs.

This just isn't the case and it shocked me. The other 2 orderlies that I work with in the office in my Gardens job (both due to leave the role soon as they wait for outside work) are showing me the ropes at the moment. As always, the game of crime story swapsies came up. Jerry willingly told me his, but Gary was more sheepish, and both are Lifers. Jerry was thin, no teeth and proudly camp which didn't seem to pose any issues around the prison as you might think.

Jerry's story involved his boyfriend, they had an argument over where to go on holiday whilst trying to book online, they didn't agree and the boyfriend ended up getting stabbed. "But it's ok," says Jerry, as "I didn't kill him". Made me feel a bit uneasy sitting next to him after hearing the story recited with such disregard.

Gary, to escape having to tell his story, went for a 'snout.' Jerry took the moment to beat his gums (literally) to divulge the juicy gossip about Gary's story. Gary, now 39, strangled his girlfriend to death when he was 17, the girlfriend was 15 and pregnant. If that wasn't bad enough, Jerry went on to tell me how he then burnt the body to try and get rid of the evidence.

It made me feel uneasy sat alone in an office with 2 individuals who are capable of such acts but were so quick to judge me and tell me their opinions on mine, I bit my tongue being with a knife attacker and a certified killer.

It's a double edged sword. Regardless of the severity of the crime, eventually they will be released and need to be prepared to do so safely back into the public, especially prisoners that have been inside for a long time. The other side of the argument, you can get someone who batters an old lady for her handbag and gets 3 years and another who gets 5 years for tax charges. The one that you'd deem as more of a risk to the public would be out mingling with the general public, in an open prison and accessing ROTLs much sooner than someone in prison for tax evasion; the system just doesn't feel right.

Things haven't got any better with James, and he gets checked daily by officers at random times due to being on suicide watch and is making no friends with the other people on the billets. He responds to their questions about his crime, which is part and parcel of bonding, with "None of your business," or thinks it's funny to answer with "I'm in prison for being a cannibal". He is already in their bad books for bringing officers to the door multiple times a day which keeps them all on their feet with phones, drugs and other contraband.

I'm struggling to sleep with feeling uneasy having him in the room, the noise of the billet and also the anxiety of possibly waking up and finding something bad has happened to James.

I've been here a month now and started to settle and get used to the regime. The novelty has also, unfortunately, started to wear off. I've done thousands of laps of the place since being here and know every inch of Ford. I'm also extremely bored of the Garden's office job. I've just seen an induction job being advertised to help new people when they arrive, so I've applied.

When I came from Wandsworth there were a few of us on the bus, we shared that experience of getting here from that hell hole and going through induction together and I got to know a few of them over time. 'D,' as everyone called him, was a well-built black guy and well respected. He was on the Violence Reduction Team at Wandsworth and got straight into the same role at Ford. Shame it didn't do him any favours.

The news of his arrival didn't take long to get round Ford. The majority were happy to see him, with a lot of previous Wandsworth residents taking him under their wings, showing him the ropes and getting him on their billet. Unluckily for him, the news of his arrival also spread to the Albanian brother which he owed money to on the outside.

Last night, just before roll check, everyone came running out of the billet across the road from us where they had been playing cards in the entrance area. The Albanian had walked on armed with a craft knife that you can buy from the Canteen, stood behind D as if to watch the card game and then stabbed him multiple times in the neck before running out the fire exit down the other end of the corridor.

D, gasping for air, stumbled out with a towel round his neck trying to curb the blood flow from his neck and collapsed into a metal trolley (used when people move property into their billet) which someone had grabbed from the billet behind and then they wheeled him to the main office next to the dinner hall to get help. He was rushed to hospital, had emergency surgery and never came back, apparently for his own safety and was moved to another Cat D upon his recovery. No one grassed on the Albanian due to fear of repercussions and he finished his sentence and left the week after.

Cat D really does seem pointless, even though I know the process is to aid people back to resettlement before release. I'm here with just under 2 years to go, and while it's miles better than Wandsworth apart from walking out the front gates, I feel like a zoo animal; I'm free to roam but not free to leave. If only the general public could see everyone in the Chapel on a Saturday night doing a weekly quiz or 11 a-side football or cricket at the weekends. Prisoners walking out of prison on Friday on a ROTL, getting the train at Ford station with the general public not knowing that they are sat right next to a prisoner, then they don't return until Tuesday, it's all a bit bizarre!

I must be cursed! Another morning waiting for the bell to go to release us, and it's late again which means they are probably going to collect people to ship out. Officers walk by our window again which makes hairs stand on end. You can hear their radio as they walk up the corridor and get nearer. The door goes yet again, "James?" Not again, I thought to myself. Out goes James, they are transferring him to Standford Hill Cat D for his own safety, mental health and wellbeing to be nearer to his mother. I must be cursed, onto my 4th cell mate in 5 weeks!

Drugs and phones in here are rifer than Wandsworth due to the ease of getting things in and chucked over the fences, plus lack of officers. Regardless of the consequences of losing ROTLs, being shipped out, going back to closed and the risk of extra time on the sentence, people just can't help themselves. About 5 people a week are being shipped back to closed now and about 2 people a week just walk out the front gate and abscond.

Today we weren't released at all for the morning session of work, and instead they compiled a search team to raid G1 and G2 billets due to security intelligence (someone's grassed). They found 16 phones and 600 Pregabalin tablets. They were hidden everywhere; under the grass outside, in the strip lighting, under the flooring, drains and even in the toilet cistern. People have become smarter taking the sim cards out when they hide the phone so if the phone is found they can't trace the activity on the phone, who they called, texted or whose number it is. I've heard a variety of places they hide the sim cards; the most inventive, someone keeps it under their foreskin, now that's a dirty call!

This evening I was completing my final laps of Ford before roll check when 3 bin liners landed right next to my heels after being lobbed over the high metal fences. Before I could even comprehend what was happening, a ninja covered head to toe in black appeared out the back of J billet and as fast as Usain Bolt, grabbed the bin liners and ran back in.

Someone I know resides on J billet, and he confirmed the contents inside the bag contained enough ingredients for a full English breakfast for the whole billet, with packs of bacon and sausages which they cooked together with their canteen tins of beans and eggs. On my next lap you could smell it a mile off as they microwaved everything and immediately to get rid of the evidence, it smelt like heaven!

Finally, I've being given a new job and got accepted for the role of Induction Orderly. Not only does it mean I can escape the mundane Gardens job, but also one of the biggest perks is that you get a priority single cell which comes with the induction billet!

There was also a big meeting today as there is a change in ROTL policy. The FLED date is being dropped. This date was when you reached half of your sentence which you are serving. For me, a 5 year sentence, I serve half, which means 2 and a half years behind bars. My FLED date is half of this time, so my FLED date is 1 year 3 months served before I can access ROTL. Now, with no FLED date, people coming to Ford only have to do a 12-week laydown (settle in period) before they can access ROTL.

Typically, this is only for new residents and is not applied retrospectively. Irritatingly, I'll be inducting people who will complete their laydown period and complete their first ROTLSs before I do! It was a real kick to the gut! This comes into effect from the 19th of February 2019, but I still need to wait until my FLED date which will be in July 2019. Gutted!

Chapter 24. OAP Bare Knuckle Boxing

8 weeks in, I've finally been offered the induction single, and luckily my friend, Matthew, who I knew from Radio Wanno at Wandsworth moved in after James for the short period until I got my single. He was due to complete his sentence in March anyway so was happy for me when I got my single room as I still had some time to go.

I moved in like a shot! The feeling of having your own space for the first time in a long time was overwhelming. It was the same size room as the one I'd come from, but just me! One bed, one wardrobe, it felt like I'd had an extension done!

I quickly made it my own by putting up pictures of my family on the walls and cupboards and giving the place a thorough clean from top to bottom and unpacked. Bliss!

P1 Billet which was a temporary place for new inductees only housed 8 residents as all the rooms were single. P2, another induction billet, housed 16 as everyone was doubled up. P1 was quiet, peaceful, serene, it made the world of difference to my mental health, happiness and wellbeing.

Now I wanted the luxuries to go with it so put the feelers out there for a cheap PS2 so I could play games and watch DVDs from the library. The "Ford Dealer" in the Q's Lifer billet had one for sale in return for a £10 packet of burn on the canteen, done deal!

Now I rent DVDs from the library 2 at a time to pass away the evenings. To take a crap without someone banging on the door asking how long I'm going to be or having to wait hours for a microwave to be free is heaven!

My wage has now gone up too. I was being pad £9.50 a week on the Gardens, but as an Orderly this goes up to £14.50 which really helps as I put the extra on phone credit. Another perk is I get 3 sessions of gym a week instead of 2. They hold special Orderly gym sessions, whichare quiet and during the day, whereas the normal evening gym sessions are rammed and you have to queue round the block!

I joined Matthew on his training routine and he put me through my paces. Treadmill full sprint for 30 seconds, rest for 30 seconds, repeat for 12 times. Then burpees, press ups, chest press. I almost puked. I started making this a regular part of my days to help breakup the mundane.

The O Billets are specifically for the over 50's to keep them away from the lively hustle and bustle of the other billets. One resident, who was quite wealthy, had a nice phone credit balance so sat most of the time on the phone to his wife, children and grandchildren. With only one phone per 16 people and everyone also wanting to speak to their loved ones in the evening, it doesn't take much for things to reach boiling point.

He could see people kept coming to check if the phone was free and instead of ending one call then waiting for others to use the phone next, he would finish one call and then start dialing to make his next 20-minute call. He wasn't to be messed with, but neither were a lot of other old school proper London gangsters, and an impromptu bare knuckle boxing match ensued outside in between the O billets.

To say they were both over 50, they went for it swinging left, right and centre with a few heavy blows landing each. Someone took the opportunity to get rid of the phone hogger and the bully of the billet and grassed them up, and both were shipped out the next day.

It must have sparked a chain reaction, as a few days later there was another incident with the 49p craft knife from the Canteen. Another argument about the billet phone, someone was hogging the phone, someone asked, someone got told to fuck off. After the phone call, he went back to his room to play his Xbox with his roommate, door the gets swung open and in he comes with a craft knife and swung for his face. Luckily, he dodged backwards and was only nicked under the chin, still enough to leave a nasty scar, everyone intervened and that was that.

He did wait till the guy took a shower later that evening to take his chance to beat the living daylights out the knife wielder.

Tess is struggling at home and Hannah is constantly having to console her. I'm now spending £20 a week on the phone to keep as much contact as I can and I write and send hand drawn pictures to my daughter daily.

She's 8 next month (April 2019). This whole ordeal started when she was 3 and we have managed to protect her from it all so far. The 3-and-a-half-year investigation, 2 month trial and nearly a year in prison but I think the time's up. People in her school have started making comments and it's unfair to leave her in the dark.

Maybe this is why she is so upset, because she knew the truth but also knew we weren't being truthful with her but she's too sensitive to say anything. We had asked her on many occasions if any of her friends or people from school had mentioned anything about daddy and her default response would be "no".

The final straw was when Tess said she cried at school when her friend came up to her and said "My brother knows your daddy is in prison." She said they both cried and hugged. It's probably time we tell her the truth so she doesn't have to suppress her feelings anymore and to know there is support there for her.

Selfishly, I didn't want her to know the truth of what I'd been through, I didn't want her opinion of me to be tarnished as she had always held me as her hero and been proud of me. How do you explain this to an 8-year-old? How do you confirm all the spiteful, horrible and nasty comments she had been hearing in the playground were actually true to some extent.

I spoke to a psychologist here in the Healthcare Department about the situation and she said that as devastatingly heartbreaking as it will be, the best way would be to bite the bullet.

Instead of blinding her with the science of it all, the injustice I felt, the ins and outs, it best for her just to comprehend that '

"I've made a mistake and that's why I'm in prison."

The next day Tess came for a visit, on a Wednesday between 6-8. She was over the moon to see me as we hadn't seen each other in over a fortnight. After she settled, I sat her on my knee, took a deep breath and I was so nervous about what I was just about to say.

"I got something to tell you as you're old enough, smart enough and deserve to know the truth". She looked excited of what was to come, yet apprehensive. "You know daddy said he was at work and that's why I couldn't come home, and you remember daddy used to run a business at home. Well, daddy made a mistake in the business and I'm in prison." I even shivered saying the word aloud, PRISON!

She looked relieved to be finally told the truth, and when I asked how she felt about it she replied, "You should have told me yesterday" in a jokey kind of adult way. What an absolutely hideous thing to have to do.

You could see instantly the change in her demeanor like a weight had been lifted. She was dancing, chatty, full of life. She did let slip that her friend's brother had told her who reported it back to Tess but didn't elaborate further than that.

The cost of prison has started to weigh heavy. £100 a month into my prison account, the cost of coming to visit, sending me stamps, spending at the shop when she comes to visit so I can take items back in with me, phone credit and cost of life on the outside for my family without my wage coming in anymore.

Did I tell you the time how the 'Fraudster' got Defrauded? The only item that was left that didn't get confiscated was my Breitling watch which they left on my desk when they raided for some reason. I was hoping to hold onto it for when I came home but with the only asset remaining, I would rather get the money from it and Hannah use it to pay for everyday expenses for her and Tess. I tried multiple times to get her to sell it, but she was adamant she wanted to hold onto it for me until eventually I convinced her otherwise.

She took it to a watch shop in town who offered £1500 which was about half the price of what I knew it was worth. Hannah also confirmed on eBay they were going for about £3000-3500. Instead, she turned to her dad to sell it online for its true value and gave it to him to take care of.

One evening, Hannah sounded so excited to share the news with me that her dad had sold it online for £3300 and the cash injection couldn't have come at a better time. The guy was coming to her dad's the next day to pick it up.

After the weekend, her dad went to the bank to collect the money to give to his daughter which the guy had bank transferred for the watch upon collection. Her dad, after asking to withdraw £3300, to his horror was declined by the bank. "Sorry sir, the cheque is yet to clear that's why its showing 2 balances; Available and Credit. You might need to wait until at least Wednesday to see if it clears". When Hannah relayed this news to me, I instantly knew we had been defrauded. The irony, the fraudster gets defrauded of a designer watch!

Someone's now walking round with my last remaining asset on their wrist and I'm £3300 out of pocket. It was a bitter pill to that we got scammed on Gumtree. Getting someone to pay in via cheque and then to bounce the cheque has to be one of the oldest scams, but obviously, Im still Gutted!

3 months in at Ford and I feel I'm on a hamster wheel now doing the same things day in day out. Bus comes in, I check them in, show them round, get them to where they need to be, gym, food, walk round, watch DVDs, bed. I'm bored out my mind.

Today's list came in, and a bus from Wandsworth was due after lunch. I looked at the names of the new arrivals and was ecstatic to see Curtis was on the list. As the bus arrived, I ran to the holding area for the emotional reunion as we embraced.

We had done the most of Wandsworth together and now we can see our similar sentences out together at Ford, it was like a new chapter had started for the better. I managed to keep Curtis on the same induction billet as me for 2 weeks and every evening we just chatted, caught up, watched films and played Colin McRae on the PlayStation. The 2 weeks flew by but eventually he had to move off and I ensured that I got him in the quieter O billet. We spent every time outside of roll checks and work together, and it made Ford just that little bit easier.

Another day, another incident, this time involving a guy called 'Manny', a very peculiar Indian fella in his early 30s. He was very OCD and had moved onto our billet as he was an Orderly for the Resettlement team.

Every day he would take all the contents out his cell, disinfect the room and then return all the contents. He had one of those old style curly moustaches, was extremely quiet and didn't really engage with the rest of the billet or anyone else.

He tried everything to get a single in the main building where the dinner hall was but hadn't been here long enough and only had entitlement to a single due to being an Orderly. Instead of taking it on the chin, he went down another route and reported that he had a conflict with someone on the billet. They didn't believe that either and moved him to the Q billet. By this time he had got under the nose of many officers and CMs.

To make his mark, Manny got his feet quickly under the table with many people on the Qs and befriending many. A few days later, the Qs turned on him, stormed his room and beat him black and blue. The next day, 5 people were shipped out and Manny returned to his old room on our billet for his own safety. His head was a mess, red welt, marks and bruising everywhere, they properly went to town on him. His head looked a different shape, he didn't venture from him room at all and we barely saw him.

Everyone in the prison was talking about it, apparently his previous sentence to the one he is serving now was a sex offence and an officer had 'accidently' left his paperwork on the Qs, so when the other residents found out they took matters into their own hands.

Manny claims it was all a big misunderstanding. He had a 15-year-old girlfriend when he was 16 and the dad reported him to the police. Regardless, everyone thinks he's a nonce (paedophile) here now and everyone automatically presumes young children. Manny was shipped out a day later. He can thank the officers for that one.

4 months at Ford, and it seems with the new ROTL policy and no FLED date, that everyone is able to access ROTLs and enjoy time out the prison while I'm the only person left in the prison that can't leave. Tess is struggling, I'm missing quality time, especially intimacy with my wife, and yet I'm still made to wait until 20th July 2019 which is still in 2 months' time.

Twice weekly, the main governor of Ford, Governor Jerry comes into the Induction hut and has a talk with the new residents of Ford. Being an Orderly, we are required to sit in these meetings too, and he has got to know me by name which will hopefully work to my advantage.

After one of his talks, I managed to talk to him to discuss my predicament with ROTLs. H e sympathised, surprisingly, and asked me to put it all in writing, provide proof of the issues with Tess and her mental wellbeing at school and he will consider using his discretion.

We managed to get a letter from the Headmistress of Tess's school, a letter from the doctors' about Hannah's PCOS and doctors notes about my mother's health. The next Governor's meeting at induction, I provided all the documentation to Gov Jerry and now I wait.

6 Months Done at Ford. Finally, after what seems a lifetime of waiting for the Governor to give me his decision, I've finally got my answer. He has approved for me to be on the same new ROTL system as everyone else.

This means I will only get ROTL a month earlier than July, but I'd take even a day earlier at this point!

I've just put in my first 2 dates for June, the first being 11th June 2019. Breaking the news to Hannah and Tess was super exciting and we partied down the phone, Hannah cried, and Tess squealed, The date couldn't come round quick enough!

Chapter 25. Interviewing a Killer

We have a few new Orderlies come and go on P1, but it's still heavenly peaceful compared to anywhere else in Ford to reside, when in moves Freddy Kraw, AKA Jock, due to being Scottish.

He had no teeth, was all gums, was tall, broad and looked like Slough from the goonies film. He worked outside part-time at Timpson's Training Academy but also as the general handyman for Ford doing painting and decorating. He was jack of all trades and had fingers in all pies. You wanted something, he could get it, want something fixing, he could mend it.

I had a hole in my coat which he sewed for me. I was handed down a CD player which was broken and he managed to fix the spindle to play disks. My room walls were tired and shabby and whilst I was walking one evening, he took it upon himself to paint and decorate my whole room which, was amazing.

However, he did have some peculiar traits. One was listening into my calls. P1 unlike L2 was peacefully quiet and I could always get on the phone which was a bonus. I'd make my final 10:30pm call at night when the billet was silent. As I start dialing the numbers, I would hear his door get wedged open and he pretends he is making his way to the kitchen behind me yet does nothing in the kitchen just so he can eavesdrop on my call. It's not me being paranoid, either, as it happens on multiple occasions. Sometimes after the call he would ask me, "Was that the wife ?" or say comments back to me in a jokey manner like "Love you," then pretend to blow kisses with his gurning gums.

It was extremely irritating and always felt like I was being listened to which made me uncomfortable when I was on the phone. I put it down to him being intrigued by what it must be like to have a normal relationship with someone on the outside as he had been behind bars for 20 years.

He also had an unhealthy obsession with the seagulls that we were plagued with at Ford; they were everywhere and so bloody noisy! He wasted a loaf of bread a day on feeding the birds which is fine, but at night he found it hilarious to lob a loaf on top of the roof so at 6am when the birds noticed bread on the roof it would sound like a stampede above your head. Funny the first time, not the tenth. He found it hilarious each and every time!

He often sits next to me on the chair as I lay on my bed and we watch a film together. One evening we got round to having a chat about his crime. He murdered someone by punching them repeatedly in the face until the head eventually caved in. I probed further what made him do it, he said because they were a 'grass'. I had been told other stories by officers I worked with in Induction that he was actually in for a hate crime, luring a gay guy he met in a chat room to a park and then he and his mate killed him, unprovoked, because of the fact he was gay.

I've often watched programmes where they interviewed murderers and killers and found it fascinating, yet here I am with one sat right next to me and I'm the one asking the questions. I asked about how it felt when he realised he had killed someone, and he said "I didn't really feel too much as it was in the heat of the moment and didn't mean for it to end up with him being dead, but it is what it is". He added he felt sorry for taking someone's life and wishes he'd been there to see his daughter (now 24) grow up.

It was an odd experience to have someone who seemed to have their heart in the right place, yet be capable of such an horrific act. He was quite graphic about how the face caved in from his fists alone (like it was going to be impressive for me to hear) and how he handed himself in, like that takes some heat off the severity of the crime, yet still carried on justifying it saying that he was a grass and in some way deserved the beating that attributed to his death. The irony is that after our chat he walked back into his room, picked up the Xbox controller and carried on killing people on his Call of Duty shooting game.

One weekend after lunch, I caught him hanging out the back fire exit door which leads straight onto the field. I'd heard him chuckling from my room as I resided on P1-04 which was right at the end of the corridor next to the fire door. He seemed to be tying chunks of bread to a piece of string. I asked him what his intentions were as he continued to bellylaugh to himself. He called Lee, the other Induction Orderly, to join us as he threw the bread attached to the string which he was clinging onto, outside the door and onto the field.

"I'm going to fly a kite," he said as we watched, and within seconds the biggest and dominant seagull swooped down and picked up the bread and flew off, or so it thought. With a mighty tug the seagull landed back onto the field. His belly went up and down as he lost his shit with laughter, his eyes were lost, and you could see the spit connecting the top and bottom gums and dribbled out his lips as he continued to reel in the seagull to within grabbing distance.

I said in an authoritative voice, "Jock, what the fuck are you playing at with this poor seagull? " but it fell on deaf ears as he continued to be in his own world of laughter and replied, "I've got plans for this one, it's going to be the most hilarious thing you've ever seen"

Mack Howard, another guy that worked in Induction, resided on P2, the billet a few feet from ours. He had just gone on a ROTL for the weekend and left the window open to his room to air it whilst he was out. Jock ran over whilst clutching the seagull and yanked the window open as far as he could before throwing the bird in and shutting the window. He shouted over like a giddy child, That bird's going to go nuts and shit all over his things".

Granted, the idea on paper was ingenious and fucking hilarious, but the reality of coming back and probably finding a dead seagull in your room and your items and bed covered in bird shit is totally off the mark for anyone's personality and humour. Luckily, someone on P2 saw what was happening and after jock disappeared, opened the window wide again for the bird to eventually escape. God only knows what must go through his mind throughout the day!

Finally, its RDR day (Resettlement Day Release). I've been so excited and waiting like a child for Christmas since putting in the ROTL paperwork. I felt excited, anxious and nervous all at the same time. In the morning I woke up so early and showered, trimmed, then started to choose what to wear for the day for the first day out of prison in over a year and 2 months.

Everyone came to my door or window to wish me well and made derogatory funny comments such as "Good luck getting your balls emptied today" or "Hope you get some", seemed to be the first thing on people's minds when you start accessing ROTLs, and I'm not surprised as everyone's sex starved.

9:30 arrived so I made my way to A Wing office to hand in my key, then off to Reception, signed my ROTL licence, copy handed to the gate house on my exit of the prison, and I was out!

I couldn't stop smiling as I crossed the road to meet Hannah in the prison car park as she waited in the car. I opened the passenger door, jumped in and we hugged, squealed, kissed and were as excited as 2 children at Christmas whilst repeating "You're out, can you believe it?!" She was beaming from ear to ear.

Down by my feet was a nice little treat, she had picked up a McDonalds breakfast on the way. Hashbrowns, bacon roll and a coke. It was the best smelling and tasting McDonalds I've had in my life. The flavours, texture and actual meat was divine! Hannah stared at me attentively as she enjoyed each bite through me as I inhaled the lot in record speed. The joy of not having to eat prison food was beyond a relief after a year and a half.

As we drove home, I just stared at her, kept hugging her and it was so bizarre to be free, albeit for the day, unrestricted, unsupervised and no longer cocooned, finally! The speed of the car felt so fast as did other cars as they zipped past us on the motorway. The pace of everything felt so much quicker and I really noticed the motion of the car as we travelled and it felt peculiar from only being in a sweatbox twice since court. The journey which was approx. 1 and a half hours went like a flash.

It was about 11am by the time we arrived home. Hannah had moved home since I was in prison, so this was the first time that I had seen the flat apart from the pictures that she sent me. As Hannah unlocked the door and led me in by the hand, it felt like a first date as she gave me a tour round the place.

All the rooms which I'd heard about multiple times on the phone I now find myself physically in the middle of, it was almost like standing in a tv set, yet this was home for my family. All the same furniture yet in different surroundings was quite surreal, but Hannah had put her own stamp on it to make it feel more like home with various trinkets and art on the walls.

We ended the tour in a pile on our bed. Our mattress compared to the blue gym matts that id been sleeping on in prison was like a cloud in comparison, I sank in and was in comfort ecstasy. We turned to each other and got passionate, but it was a little awkward like it was our first time with it being so long since we were last able to do anything.

After working up an appetite, there was one other craving that needed fulfilling, Nando's!

Being back out with the public was an uncomfortable experience, and I kept having thoughts about what if people recognised me, what would I say if someone approached, how would I handle it. It quickly subsided when I took the stance that I don't actually give a shit and I needed to savour every moment with my wife.

I hadn't arranged a locker yet with the prison so didn't have a mobile phone at the table, and it was quite liberating to be totally engaged with no distractions whilst I demolished the most beautiful and delicious Nando's that's ever touched my lips. The experience of just us 2 and the food was magical, like nothing else in the world mattered at that exact moment.

We chatted and bonded until it was time to get Tess from school. She knew I was coming to pick her up and was at the door of her classroom, and like a dog out the traps she ran full pelt when she saw me. I scooped her up, twirled her around in pure bliss and reunited with my wife, the Hockey tribe were back together again.

The afternoon was all her choice, whatever she wanted to do. "Football" she shouted so we bought her a brand-new rainbow ball from the shop, parked up at a field, she took one mighty kick and out of nowhere a dog ran towards it, grabbed it in its mouth and popped it. Tess bawled her eyes out. Not the best start! Back in the car, back to shop and back to another field, she wouldn't leave my side and forgot we were meant to be playing football.

When we got home, she proudly gave me another tour and I had to pretend it was the first-time I'd seen it, then she wanted to play hide and seek, then playfight, watch

YouTube videos and before I knew it, our time was up and I had to get back.

Luckily my mother offered to pick me up and return me to Ford prison so at least we could have a good chat and my wife didn't have to drive all the way there and back again. It was extremely tough saying goodbye after having a taster of what your life should be like, but instead, I'm off to hand myself back into prison. Hannah was distraught and couldn't stop crying, Tess too. Driving away at 7:30pm felt like day one all over again when I left to go and get sentenced, a real kick to the stomach. Our next ROTL is in 10 days' time, but it still did nothing to ease the pain.

On the way back, Tess Facetimed me on my mother's phone, she was all puffy eyed and was distraught that I'd gone and both of them felt empty. It killed my heart as she blubbered down the phone that she misses me.

My sister, Sam, also came along for the journey to keep my mum company on the return leg. The conversations were all about stories of Wandsworth, Ford and what I'd done today and before long, I was stood back outside the prison which looked like a zoo from the outside with its high green metal fencing.

Walking back into prison was awful! It was so strange voluntarily (but obliged) to walk myself back into a prison was demoraliaing. I made my way back to the billet, everyone was away as last roll check had already been done, the place was eerily desolate and quiet. Back in my room, I shut my door and it dawned on me like a ton of bricks how shit and basic my life really is, the ridiculous amount of time left (I'm only halfway through my sentence) and how much I love and miss my family.

As I lay on my uncomfortable bed, in the most basic box room, basically in a glorified shed in the middle of a field, I felt so so alone, homesick, depressed and felt empathy for my girls struggling at home without me.

For days after the ROTL, everything felt so pointless like a total waste of time, I just kept thinking of my taster of life on the outside and what I'm missing. It really fucked with my mind as you get into a routine in prison then a taste of normality then ripped away and thrown back into a terrible environment with terrible people and the awful routine you have to follow. It was not only emotionally but mentally challenging.

Chapter 26. A Hitman at Ford

I've just come back from my first ROR (Resettlement Overnight Release). I was given 3 days and 2 nights at home due to it being my first and it increases with each one that you complete. Tess gave me a guided tour once again and had put up all the pictures that I had drawn for her over my time in prison all over her wardrobes and was so proud to show me.

It is amazing how quick you are able to adapt back to normal life at home like nothing ever happened. Even though we had 3 days, the first half a day was travelling back home and so was the final day. The rest of the time I found myself clockwatching, trying to make the most out of each and every second. We baked cakes, played with her guinea pigs, built her a 6ft trampoline, football, swimming, she named it, we did it. Once she had gone to bed from being knackered from the day's activities, me and the wife were able to enjoy some alone adult time which was overwhelming.

Even though you're not meant to drink on ROTLs, we enjoyed a bottle of Prosecco between us and watched Netflix and chatted until the early hours.

The prison has a rule that you are allowed to bring property back to the prison within the guidelines and preapproved, once every 3 months. I took full advantage and Hannah had made sure she provided everything on a list that I had sent her in the post. Stereo, rug, 10 DVDs, 10 CDs, portable Dab radio, electric toothbrush, clothing and thermos water bottle. She's been so good to me throughout all of this and trying to make my life as comfortable as possible through the worst time of my life, bless her.

The 3 days went like a flash, we tried to stay strong as we drove towards the prison after one of the most amazing weekends together as a family. As I loaded up all my new goodies to take back in, piled up like a work horse, it hit everyone again like a brick wall that I would soon be gone. Tess clung to my leg, Hannah was hugging me whilst sobbing and I welled up as we said our goodbyes once more and peeled myself away to head on back into the Reception of the prison once more.

Coming back from RDRs had been tough, even more so when you've stayed for days. You get even more settled, even more used to normal life and back into being part of your family. Just as you're getting comfortable, you're ripped apart and slung back into prison, it's devastating for everyone to deal with and is mentally challenging.

We always thought ROTLs would be a game changer and ease the pain of prison and time apart. However, we were never prepared to deal with the constant highs and lows that come with them and how it makes you crash back down to earth when you come back. It takes a good few weeks to get your head back into the game, then you start to look forward to the next one, then the process starts all over again.

I must have timed this ROTL pretty well, the prison was buzzing with the newest drama that unfolded over the weekend whilst I was away. The security even to get back into the prison was tighter and I thought it was unusual that the gates to the front gate were locked and my next-door neighbor, Mr Bush was missing.

Bush had been inside for about 14 years for a £30million armed robbery with most of the money still missing. He had just completed his first supervised RDR a few days before I left before receiving bad news that his next one had been suspended due to a security warning.

I remember overhearing his conversation with his solicitor down the phone that he had been given threats throughout his sentence and they were all bollocks and it's just the police trying to stop him going out etc.

Turns out the police were actually doing him a favour as they had been given a tip off that a hit had been put on him and his accomplices. Bush's co-defendant and the co-defendant's daughter were machine gunned down in the house they rented from comedian Russel Kane.

It dawned on me the serenity and timing of me not being here this weekend. The hit man could have easily walked into Ford undetected as its literally open, people come and go all day due to having to leave the prison and cross the road to go to work in the gardens.

If the gunman walked in looking for Bush, the lack of officers and security, the billets pretty much being made out of cardboard and me being next door, if he opened fire, it would have been too close for comfort! it isn't just me over dramatising it either, it was a realistic possible and they even shipped Bush back to closed conditions for his own safety.

There's so many people being shipped out of Ford now for silly things. I don't know why people risk it and go back to closed conditions, I guess the temptation is too much for some.

A lot of empty busses came today and parked outside of the block. Apparently, the block only holds 4 to 5 people but was double the capacity. Last night some hungry residents decided to get a Chuckeroo delivery, the 11 herbs and spices were just too good to resist and the KFC was chucked over the fence in some binbags.

The officer night patrol was in the right place at the right time and a game of KFC rugby ensued. The salivating KFC bandits were caught red-handed and upon raiding the billet, found further greasy fingered participants with the bin looking like a graveyard full of bones from an earlier delivery. Near enough the whole billet was shipped out, all for a KFC!

CRL License, The Get out of Jail Free Card! I had heard through the grapevine that you can apply to have extra ROTLs via a CRL license if you have children. A CRL is a 'Childcare Resettlement Licence' and is for the purpose of maintaining ties between parent and child. One caveat though, you need to be a primary carer.

I found this statement in itself quite ambiguous as how can you be a primary carer if you're in prison? Whoever you left your child with, whether it be a grandparent or partner, surely they would now be the primary carer? Anyway, I decided to apply. You can get a maximum of another 3 days and 2 nights at home. Worth a shot! I included ever piece of information that I had; school letters, medical notes, the fact my child was struggling due to me being in prison.

It wasn't easy. It took about a month, a few declines and me pushing OMU (Offender Management Unit) about the wording of the document before they eventually granted me an extra 12hour RDR instead of a CRL. I still took them to task on it, they agreed in the end but said they would rather give me a 'Special Circumstances Discretionary RDR' rather than a CRL because, in their exact words, 'Everyone would want one' if they granted it to me.

Only one person in Ford is currently accessing a CRL, he is a dad to 3 and no mother around, the grandmother had been looking after the children in his absence, so they deemed this suitable to grant a CRL.

Well, it's a bonus, nothing ventured nothing gained, getting another 12 hours out of this place a month on top of my RORs is a huge win in my eyes!

13 long months left now and the time ahead has never felt so apparent. Calling back home today was like speaking to the dead. Both Hannah and Tess had caught the Norovirus, and both were violently being sick and had diarrhea over the past 24 hours.

My wife was crying down the phone as she tried to cater to Tess's needs whilst she needed looking after herself. She was pining for me down the phone and crying with the exhaustion and illness. I felt so powerless and just wanted to help but there was nothing at all that I could do apart from lend my ear to her down the phone.

I tried to ask OMU for an SPL (Special Purpose Licence) to go and look after them, but they didn't even get back to me. I've since learnt they only grant these if someone is terminally ill or if you need to attend a funeral. I'd have done anything to get home to look after my sick family, but this wasn't seen in their eyes as an emergency! It felt unfair, irritating and disgusting that my family are suffering at home and I'm just stuck here wandering around in this pointless existence!

Its amazing what you find out people have been saying about you whilst you're inside prison. People who you thought had your back end up being backstabbers once you're incarcerated.

My uncle, who I looked up to like a dad figure (with my own dying when I was about 17). Since being in prison, I have not received so much as one email, letter or even £10 put in my prison account. He hasn't checked on my wife, daughter or even attempted to visit. I confided to him and his wife on many occasions around the dinner table and explained, at length, the case in full and all of its complexities and accusations.

It cut deep to hear from my own mother through a letter, what had been said behind my back. "It's because he didn't pay his taxes which is the reason he got done, don't pay your taxes you deserve to go to prison". Paying tax back to the tax man had nothing to do with my case!

I felt such a fool, kept playing the memories of explaining everything round the table to those who I believed had my back and total faith in me, my best interests at heart and unconditional support. Then as soon as my back was turned, they were laughing, sneering and jeering at me and every time I poured my heart out, it all fell on deaf ears.

It didn't stop there, my mother also went to a BBQ and mocked my situation, proudly shouting in front of everyone where's your middle child (I've got 2 sisters) "oh yeah, he's in prison", then continued to make similarities between a small space stating, "This is probably about the same size as his cell". Nice to know I'm highly thought of in my absence.

Next it was the turn of my cousin, bearing in mind I've not seen him since we were about 15 years old. He trolled all articles and Facebook comments stating, "This is my so-called cousin who I'm ashamed to be associated with, can't believe what he's done". What is it with people wanted to jump on the tail end of something popular to big up their own ego with associating themselves with me contradicting what his post is actually saying?

Chapter 27. Inducting a Terrorist

How typical, they have just changed the policy in regard to Cat D eligibility. Previously you could only come to a Cat D if you had less than 24 months remaining on your sentence, but they have now increased this to 30 months! I always just seem to have missed out; I could have had such a shorter stay at Wandsworth if this had been the case about a year ago.

I've completed many RORs now, but it still gets harder to live month by month. We play fake happily families for 5 days then traumatically and sadistically, reality kicks back in, I'm back at Ford and they are alone with the ghost of me still lingering until we get used to me being gone again.

Previously, in my normal life before prison, if I was told at a pub that 'the guy at the bar is a murderer', I would have given them a wide birth. Now, after meeting and inducting so many, it still baffles me how complacent I've got with it all. I suppose you have no choice but to adapt, especially when my job is to induct these individuals. Some Lifers come here after spending years, if not decades locked up behind bars and it can be a shock to the system to all of a sudden have so much freedom.

I've noticed the same traits in a lot of them; dead behind the eyes, empty inside, focus on the inanest of things and they are often very needy. They have had years of being told what to do and at what time for so long by officers that now, you need to stand on your own two feet without the comfort blanket, becomes a struggle for some.

There isn't much here in the way of helping such individuals adapt and it falls on us prisoners, the induction team, to take the pressure of helping them adjust, but its draining! They have so many needs, they demand rather than talk, make it extremely uncomfortable when their demands can't be met and it's hard not to be judgmental when you've been told their crimes.

A few examples. Liam, in for stabbing his mate in the neck during an argument after a drug and booze filled evening, then went and buried his body in the morning. Jim strangled his wife to death. Pete killed and buried his wife under a hospital he was helping to build at the time. Dave, a one punch wonder, knocked the guy out who hit the floor and instantly died. Warren stabbed his victim 22 times and disemboweled them, Jim who was high on drugs went on a zombie knife killing spree and finally Phil, who strangled his Grandson.

To top it all off, this week we have had the highest security warning we have ever had in Ford. Abdul Kaylil, who had already served 20 years, was a thin Osama Bin Laden looking guy who was in for terrorism charges. The Parole Board sent him here before they will consider him for Parole, and I thought Cat D was supposed to be for low-risk prisoners? It is scary to think these people, in a matter of a small few years or less, will be released from prison. The whole prison is on high alert due to Abdul's arrival, and the whole prison is talking about the terrorist at Ford, He hasn't come out of his room at all or come to any of the induction sessions.

We were tasked on many occasions to go check on his welfare; the guy was friendly enough, oddly, but when he talked to you it was as though he was talking straight through you as if he was talking to your soul. Ironically, he didn't venture out from his room due to fears for his own safety.

The terrorist's stay at Ford was short lived, however. Today, 29th November 2019, on the news were reports of another terrorist attack on London Bridge. A radicalised ex-prisoner was released at halfway through his 16-year sentence after appealing his IPP sentence, he wasn't out long before he stabbed people on London Bridge. He attacked 5 people with 2 being fatally wounded. This all took place at the prisoner "Learning Together" event at Fishmonger's Hall, next to Waterloo Bridge. A Cat D prisoner from Standford Hill was there on ROTL and helped stop the attack, as did an ex-prisonerr and a member of the MoJ).

A few days later, Abdul was shipped out back to closed conditions. How he made his way here in the first place I'll never know. It was scary having him here and rubbing shoulders with a convicted terrorist and the thoughts of the devastation that he would have caused if he hadn't been jailed.

Working in Induction I got friendly with the officers and one leaked the information to me about the terrorist; it turns out he was part of a terrorist gang that planned bomb plots in the UK and USA. So happy he is gone.

Unfortunately, the MOJ (Ministry of Justice) stopped all ROTLs immediately overnight and the gates to all open prisons were closed immediately. The prison has taken a nosedive with the capacity now being constantly full due to no one going home or to work. Food is terrible, the prison is messy and the atmosphere is restless.

11 months remaining and I'm struggling with doing the same shit every day. There's no external work being advertised for me to apply for, still not ROTLs and there's contraband everywhere. Every Thursday is Drug Result Day where they have the results back from people's piss tests, and you can guarantee at least 4 people will be leaving on these failed results alone. Due to the terrorist attack, the security has stepped up, people are being checked when they come back from work and they have started targeting troublesome residents.

Today on a security raid, as well as the likely items you'd expect to find such as food, drink, phones, steroids and drugs, worryingly they also found a Zombie knife. The guy had been working outside at the Suez recycling plant and apparently had found it that day. Frighteningly though, what was the intention of bringing it back into Ford? I used to think this was a safe place but the number of gangs, increased tension and events that keep happening make me feel uneasy as I finish my last stretch here.

10 months, 2 weeks left and I've just been approved for my Christmas ROR dates. Everyone who applies and gets accepted get 4 days, 3 nights at home starting on Xmas Eve.

I'm extremely excited to not miss another Christmas due to prison and have the opportunity to see Tess open her Christmas presents. I've also just been accepted for external employment at a company called Farplants. It's a gigantic nursery on a humongous scale and I'll be loading trolleys with the plant orders for a network of nurseries.

It's not my dream job but it gets me out of here daily and puts some money in my pocket ready for my release. The biggest bonus of all is I get to have my mobile phone with me and will be able to Facetime my family on my breaks and after work before I come back to Ford. It will also save me a fortune on phone credit on these extortionate phones in prison!

My next battle will be to get the 40% levy removed which they apply to your wages. This is imposed through something called the "Prisoners' Earnings Act" and the money deducted by the Ministry of Justice goes directly to support victims of crime. Working all day for £4 an hour, I don't think so! Hopefully, I can put another application in to Gov Jerry and he will use his discretion as a parting gift due to the hard work and late hours I've put in during my Induction Job. I've heard that he routinely waives the deduction in the last 3 or 4 months anyway, so that men can leave with some reasonable money saved. This is a lifeline with being in prison for so long and a lot of prisoners have nothing to help with resettlement when they eventually leave prison. I definitely needed to get some money behind me!

It's increasingly frustrating to see the majority of people that I've known or inducted leave the prison before me, it really shows the length of the sentence that I was handed down. As hard as I try to stay happy for the person leaving as their journey is over, a little bit more of me dies on the inside through sheer jealousy.

I had spent the summer with a guy called Ryan who was a tubby but friendly guy who kept himself to himself. He was also in for Fraud after intercepting people's payments before they hit the stock market.

We had walked round the prison together chewing the fat 100s of times. Me, Curtis, Ross and Ryan would play board games out on the field, he baked cakes for us all and when he was due to leave on HDC (Home Detention Curfew), it was gutting to lose yet another friend, or so I thought.

Curiosity got the better of me when he left and I put his name into Google when on a ROTL, only to discover he was only a dirty copper from the MET Police. The article detailed how he cashed some dead guy's cheque book to fund a gambling addiction. I couldn't believe it, I felt defrauded! He was an undercover police officer this whole time. We spoke at length of our hate for the police and he was one the whole time! Shows you that you can be anyone in prison.

When I came back from work, I came back to a new neighbour, Oscar Wheely. The guy was lovely, calm, short and thin, late 20s and was really polite and friendly.

The normal introductions of what got you into prison didn't happen which rang alarm bells. What I did find out about him after our conversation, is that he's a family man, got a young wife, 1 child who he adores and was a kitchen fitter. It was like trying to piece together a puzzle, like a real-life game of Cluedo.

A mutual acquaintance was more than happy to divulge the information. Oscar was a kitchen fitter, but also a big-time gambler. After fitting a kitchen for a wealthy client, he noticed money going in and out of a safe whilst doing the install.

A few days after completion, he went back to the house in a boiler suit and at knife point made the client open the safe. She had only just banked the cash that day, so he made away with only £500. After spending so much time with him, giving directions of how she wanted her kitchen, she recognised him and his voice and he got 9 years!

I didn't know how to feel about my new next-door neighbour. A moment of madness for 9 years (never been in trouble before), the gambling addiction took hold and changed his life forever but on the other hand the poor woman and her life has been changed forever and the mental torture she must have and still be going through.

Chapter 28. More Deliveries Here Than Amazon

Walking round each evening, you can see the chuckeroo deliveries coming over the fence and each billet has their own specialty. If you want a Jack Daniels and a dance, got to J Billet, want to be as spaced out as a horse on a vets table on Ketamine, got to K Billet. Get high and listen to some Bob Marley, got to the Qs and if you fancy a KFC or other takeaway, got to the M Billet. There are more deliveries here than Amazon!

It happens so often that the screws can't keep up with it. The funniest part was that one officer on an evening shift rang a local takeaway, and when he gave the prison address for it to be delivered to, the delivery driver asked what fence they wanted it chucking over!

One day, someone that I inducted and got along with shouted to me from the billet kitchen window. I walked in and you could smell the grease from the fried chicken they had freshly lobbed over the fence, it smelt like heaven. He had saved me a chicken leg. I've never gorged and gnawed a piece of chicken to the bone like I did during this magical moment. The flavours, the 'real' chicken, the salivation party that was going on in my mouth will never be replicated again. I was, however, constantly looking over my shoulder not to get caught red handed with greasy fingers!

Its nearly Christmas, Luckily, the ROTLs are going ahead for Christmas after the hype of the Waterloo Bridge terror attack had died down. Its Xmas Eve and 250 people who have been approved to go on their Christmas RORs make their way to the dining hall to get out for Christmas.

It was the biggest shambles I've ever seen. Everyone's licence started at 8:30, but at 8:15 there was no sign of anyone going anywhere and people started to get apprehensive as mentally they already had one foot out of the prison.

Finally, a CM turned up and instead of diffusing the rising temperature, he shouted "No-one will be going anywhere without a General App with the best landline number we can contact you on". There was a stampede to the 2 places where the General Application forms lived. Fully grown men were running to try and get there first and watching 200+ people trying to squeeze through small door frames was a sight. It was a circus created for no reason.

As soon as the first few people rushed back with what they thought was their golden ticket, they split everyone into groups anyway based on surname and processed everyone as slowly as possible like another silly power trip. I just sat back and watched it all unfold as it was too much to even watch let alone join in.

They eventually put general apps on each table anyway and after I filled mine in and waited for the crowd to disperse, I was out by 9am. The contrast to last year, banged up for Christmas, this year I'm out, it was an immense feeling of relief. My mother picked me up from the gate and I really was driving home for Christmas!

Tess was so excited to have me home and the impending arrival of Santa, it didn't matter about presents, just being home with my wife and daughter was enough, although Tess couldn't wait to open the presents nestled under the tree.

The fridge was bulging with all my favourite goods courtesy of my wife and we were both ecstatic to spend Christmas together. It is hard to be fully invested in the moment as things will trigger the fact that this is only temporary and within a few days we are back to being apart but we try snap each other out of it.

We visited each other's mums in turn and played Christmas games and ate so much buffet food I could burst. Getting home, we put Tess to bed to prepare for the big day. There is no other feeling like it, finally getting into my own marital bed with my wife, my daughter next door all cozy in her bed safe and sound and being able to enjoy Christmas tomorrow as a family was a euphoric feeling.

Christmas morning, the floorboards creaked, the door opened and in her soft high-pitched voice "HE'S BEEN!" referring to the sack of gifts that appeared at the end of her bed. I sat with Hannah and watched in delight as Tess opened all of her presents, hugging each one and thanking us every time she opened one.

It was like an out of body experience to be able to enjoy this moment but knowing inside, I'm still technically a prisoner whilst watching Tess have the time of her life.

I felt crushed and inadequate, annoyed and embarrassed that I had absolutely nothing for Hannah. The first time in 10 years. Yes, we had agreed beforehand not to get each other anything this year but seeing a conveyor belt of goods head in Tess's direction and not being able to give my wife a gift due to the situation was soul destroying.

At the end of Tess's mammoth gift opening session, Hannah pulls out a little box and passes it in my direction, a gesture as she calls it. A bloody Apple Watch, the watch I'd been after for a little while. Although second hand, it was in pristine condition and I'd be able to use it whilst working at Farplants to send voice notes and receive text messages whilst I worked. Due to having nothing, losing everything, I was so appreciative of the gesture, the gift and the sentimental value of the present.

Mother came around in the afternoon for Christmas dinner and Tess had another mound of presents to open including her main one which was a soundbar for her TV. We had brought her an Amazon Firestick so that she could watch YouTube and stream films to her TV, and now she had decent sound to go with it. She also got a 3-wheel scooter, and whilst Hannah cooked the dinner, me and mum took her on a test ride so she could have a good go, she was having the time of her life and so was I!

Christmas went like a blink of an eye and before I knew it, it was the 27th of December 2019 and I had to go back by 5:30pm. I had to catch the early train from Southampton to ensure I was back on time. We stopped at 5guys next to the train station, had some lunch and they dropped me outside and we said a very painful and emotional goodbye as I went to hand myself back into hell, yet again. My mind, soul and heart were still at home, yet my human body was walking through the gates of Ford.

They were heavy handed at Reception, which was unusual, but clearly thinking everyone will be returning with illicit items or come back pissed. Everyone was breathalyzed and 10 officers filled the room completing pat downs, metal scanners and rummaging through all property like a fine-tooth comb.

Even though they had amnesty boxes on the desk, you could see what was happening from the back of the queue so no one should get caught out. However, one guy was stupid enough to hand his coat over with £160 tucked into the secret, not so secret, pocket. He was removed immediately.

In total, 2 people came back late, 4 people failed the Breathalyzer and they caught the guy with the money. That was it. They were bitterly disappointed thinking they were going to find a lot more.

It's New Year's Eve and I can't wait for the clocks to turn so that I can finally say "I'M OUT THIS YEAR!". Another event I won't have to repeat again, but yet another event where I should be with my family!

The Governor had agreed for a little music to be played in the Chapel before last roll check. As normal, I was doing laps with Curtis to pass the time and we were about 20 feet from the chapel when we could feel the bass and hear the music as we approached like we were approaching a nightclub!

Curiosity got the better of us and we opened the door to the Chapel. Inside it was pitch black, the music hit us as did the disco lights straight in the eyes. It was a full-on drum and bass rave. They had rigged a pair of decks and mixer up to the PA system they used in church right at the back of the hall. People were bobbing their heads to the music whilst others fully embraced it and pretended they were at a gig.

The irony was hilarious, God really is a DJ. The only thing that popped into my head was, I wish I could record this, it would go viral! If only the public saw the person they thought was locked behind bars in somewhere like Wandsworth was actually having a full-blown rave up in a church, The Sun newspaper would have this as front-page news!

Its 2020, just a glance at the success and achievement finally making it into the year that I get to go home, then the excitement soon fades and reality kicks in that it's just another day, another day without my wife and child and another day incarcerated.

Finally had a response from the Governor, and he has agreed to waiver the 40% levy! What a bonus! Shows it's always worth making friends with the right people, even though a lot of people like to maintain a "Them and Us" situation regarding the divide between prisoners and officers.

The atmosphere is uneasy, but I put it down to post Christmas blues and everyone trying to get back into the swing of things after tasting some normality of being home with their loved ones.

Today I saw someone that I inducted last week, a really lovely young guy with a great temperament and quiet. He was walking round with a battered face and a slash across his chin to lip, a case of mistaken identity.

His own roommate and accomplice had been paid £250 to beat him up with the caveat they slice his face too. He had been targeted due to stealing a pair of this guy's trainers from a previous prison, a prison this guy had never been to! I still can't get over the fact he had the audacity to do that to his own roommate for just £250 and then the balls to sleep in the same room as the guy afterwards like nothing had happened is disgusting.

People have now started walking round in groups and gangs and the place has an uneasy feel about it, I've stopped walking round as much as I did as the uncomfortable feeling is unbearable.

8 months left; I've started working outside the prison at Farplants. Not only am I out every day earning, I'm also able to Facetime Tess and Hannah every day which is a huge bonus.

The majority of people that work here are of foreign nationality, Polish, Lithuanian and Albanian. I got speaking to one of them and they said they do seasons here as even at £8.25, its three times above the average of what they can earn in their home country.

The work is extremely labor intensive, it's a struggle to keep up with their graft at first and we are expected after a week to match their workload.

The work is, simply put, packing trays and pots of flowers onto rollers, but this is on an industrial scale. On one side of the factory it may require 16 pots of daffodils and on the other side of the factory 10 trays of tulips. Once you've cleared your whole trolley, you need to go back and get another one. Everything you do you have to scan to ensure it goes in the right place and to the right customer, it also means they can track your work performance.

People are regularly pulled up about their performance and even a whole group got fired and sent back to Ford due to not pulling their weight. They are extremely busy but get cheap labor from us and the foreigners who they send home at lunch time then keep us prisoners on to finish the job.

We had to sign a waiver due to the number of hours we are required to do each day, 14hour shifts are not unusual as we are made to complete the day's orders before we go back to Ford. Companies like Waitrose get their orders from Farplants and when its occasions like Mother's Day or Easter, the orders go through the roof. I really needed the money and was losing more and more dignity each time id have to ask family or friends to put money in my prison account.

Every 3 hours we get a 30-minute break. It's backbreaking work and by the time we get back to Ford, I get straight to sleep and am up early the next day to do it all again. Regardless of the manual labor, I am so glad to get out the prison and the induction job. I'd got sick of needy, rude, selfish, inconsiderate and aggressively mannered prisoners.

I'd done the induction job now for well over a year and even got to the stage of being able to predict how the new arrivals would behave based on which prison they arrived from.

Wandsworth, Brixton and Portland; the prisoners would be thankful to be at Ford, excited to be here and open to everything the prison has to offer and glad to be out of their previous prison.

Thameside, Rochester and The Mount, which are C Cat prisons with less bang up, more than likely they had a single cell, comfortable setup, job and routine but now they need to share a room, go through boarding again to access ROTL, new job, new unfamiliar environment, and a lot even ask to go back to their previous prison.

Being away from the prison due to work also meant I was away from most of the drama, which was nice. When I returned, the other residents on the induction billet would fill me in with what had been going on, the nickings and who had been shipped out.

Today, someone got shipped out for being caught selling internet access. They had brought back a 4G wireless router and had stuck it in the cavity wall on their billet. They were then selling the Wi-Fi code to people with phones and Xbox's so that they could stream films, tv programs and Xbox online. Ingenious! Until someone grassed and they went to kick him out.

I had just made it back in time to see it all unfold as they went to take this big Viking-looking bloke down the Block. He swatted them off like flies (turns out he was a cage fighter) and a biter; one female officer got bit on the arm as they bundled and tried to pin him down. First time I've seen them get the handcuffs and leg restraints out. People were cheering and laughing at so many officers go over in the scuffle.

Due to the increase in violence, illicit items and bad behavior at Ford, they have started to use ROTLS as ammo in their fight back. People are losing their RDR and RORs for the silliest thing.

One guy had his room spun and they found Beecham's tablets which he bought whilst working outside due to having a cold. He got an IEP and lost that month's ROTL. Another was for wearing a black coat, another for being found in the kitchen of the billet making dinner after 12 at night, he got an IEP and again, lost his ROTL. They even gave one to someone for not attending their doctor's appointment.

They are dishing IEPS out like sweets but not taking into consideration that it's the families and children that are suffering due to their power trip and taking away that person's ability to maintain their family ties which they say reduce reoffending.

Chapter 29. Corona Virus

I hate work, I didn't finish until 11:30pm last night and was required in at 7am this morning. I didn't get to sleep until 1am by the time I got back to the prison and had to get up at 6am the next morning to get on the prison bus ready to be taken to Farplants.

If you start to show any signs of fatigue due to tiredness, it shows in your figures of how many plants you're packing an hour, then the Polish lady who is the team manager comes straight over to crack the whip to tell you that you need to speed up. I'm hating it.

I've just been paid £650 for 88hrs work. I'm so lucky not to have to pay that 40% levy like others from my prison who averaged out £400 for the same amount of work, it just wouldn't be worth it.

The more ROTLs that I complete, the more comfortable and natural it feels to be home, the harder it is to leave and come back, it's getting mentally tougher each and every time. It's even harder with the fact that all I seem to do is sleep at Ford and go on ROTLs so what is the point of it all.

All this seems to be doing now is affecting me and my family life whilst maintaining the public perception that I'm still 'Locked Up' for my serious and dangerous crime of my conviction of 'Fraud'. If they could only see that I'm out the prison most days from 7am till 9pm, not in an environment like Wandsworth that stereotypically people picture when they think you're in prison and every other weekend I'm out either on an RDR or a 5 Day ROR. It's completely pointless, costing the government to keep me at Ford and the taxpayer.

March 2020, and today I'm 35. This all started when I was 29 and I've not celebrated a birthday since, as much as my wife has tried to make the day special. This year the world seems to want to celebrate my birthday with a pandemic of Coronavirus.

Everyone has gone mad buying toilet roll, pasta and hand sanitizer. The news and media are reporting 86,000 cases so far worldwide and 9 deaths in the UK. It's expected that the peak of the virus should hit within the next 10 weeks and hopefully reduce by summer like the flu.

Its pandemonium in the prison, and the rumours have started flying round that we will all be returned to closed conditions or the gates will be locked, Ford will be turned into a closed prison and our ROTLs will be pulled soon to stop the spread.

Being the chancers that they are, people who are on ROTLs already have called the prison to say they have come down with a cough or cold and need to isolate for 14 days as per the government guidance. The prison is not playing ball and are demanding they return immediately or they breach their ROTL and have their details passed to the police to return them to prison.

Others inside the prison have come forward saying their cell mate on the billet has symptoms to try and jump the list to get a single. It worked the first time, until the Head of Residence went to check on the guy's welfare to find the guy who had been moved to a single back with his old cell mate playing the Xbox together.

I'm just waiting now until the first reported case of coronavirus gets reported in the prison and due to the close proximity of everyone, it would spread like wildfire.

Signs have gone up all round the prison estate about handwashing and non-alcoholic hand sanitizer pumps were dotted around the place which soon went missing. People don't wash their hands after taking a shit let alone throughout a pandemic; I sit on the loo myself and hear handfuls of people come in and piss and not wash their hands, now these same people will become super spreaders, lovely.

Even though they are trying to educate and reduce the transmission inside the prison, the officers are taking no precautions and act like nothing is happening. They are the ones that will be bringing it in from the outside when they inevitably close the gates.

March 21st, 2020. It had been in the balance all week whether ROTLs would be still going ahead this weekend and as the days went on, my hopes were less and less but some miracle I got out on my 5-day ROTL.

When I got out the gates knowing this may be my last ROTL, I was elated! I couldn't have timed my ROTL any better to be back home with my loved ones whilst the pandemic unfolded.

By Monday March 23rd 2020, the number of people diagnosed with Corona was spiking and the death rate rising. We watched the TV that evening with a special news broadcast stating that the UK would be going into full lockdown with immediate effect, to stay home and to go out only for 30mins exercise or to get food whilst maintaining a 2m distance.

Being home under house arrest conditions, Tess was in her element. We played hide and seek, play fight, watched YouTube videos, baked, painted and played board games. To spend this much quality time together was amazing.

I was due back to Ford on Wednesday, and on Tuesday evening we had a call from the prison asking how I was feeling as I was due back tomorrow. The call was very unusual and peculiar like it had some type of hidden meaning, they don't normally call you on ROTLs.

Time to think quick on my feet; do I say, "Yes I'm fine thank you" or knowing the symptoms of corona virus after reading up on the virus, do I try and get extra time with my family due to the unfortunate situation with the country being in full lockdown?

In the next room was my wife who had actually been able to be genuinely happy for a limited time whilst I've been back, my daughter who cried herself to sleep last night with the anxiety of me going back tomorrow and leaving once again. I blurted out "Unfortunately, I think I've picked up a cold as my nose keeps running and I've got a bit of a temperature and can't stop coughing". I'd made my choice and what was the worst that could happen, they still want me back tomorrow and I have to isolate? Or, the other flip of the coin is I get extra time to stay at home and isolate. I took the gamble.

She said she would call me back with instructions. An hour later I received a call to say, "Right, we are extending your ROTL licence for a further 7 days for you to self-isolate at home". I couldn't get in the other room quick enough to let out the news. We all danced and jumped round the room, the excitement, joy, relief that I didn't have to leave them tomorrow and we get more quality time together.

This would be the most time that we had spent together in 2 years! Tess was beaming from ear to ear and Hannah had tears running down her face with sheer happiness. The evenings we were able to have as a couple were amazing, we were able to watch boxsets, thoroughly enjoy the evening without the feeling it was our last and to be able to put Tess to bed and be there for her in the morning was magical.

The week flew by and made the feeling of going back to prison just like the first time. Tess, now being nearly 9, knew as it was coming to an end and I needed to go back, and she would go within herself and a shell of a girl and start distancing herself from me for self-preservation.

It had got to the stage with Tess that no words could give comfort anymore, each time I was due to go back she was a mess. We would try to make her see it's only 6 months left and she would respond "Yes I know" with irritability.

It was the penultimate day before my extended licence ran out, and I was dreading going back tomorrow. The prison rang once again, with "How are your symptoms now?" Well, what would you have done? My wife answered the call. "He's currently in bed with flu-like symptoms". I know how the story of the boy who cried wolf goes, but would you rather say you have a cold or do another week in prison?

"Ok, well we are instructing you to stay at home for another 7 days on extended licence", another mini lockdown party for 3 took place in the living room! The best part is I'm here for Tess's 9th birthday on the 2nd of April. I spent her 7th birthday in court, 8th birthday in prison, finally I get to physically be there for her birthday!

It was a joy to be part of decorating the lounge in the evenings ready for her to burst through the door with excitement in the morning. She woke up the happiest I've ever seen her and woke us up shouting "IT'S MY BIRTHDAY!". I soaked up every second watching her face beam as she made all her little comments like "oh wow" and "I love it" to every gift that she opened.

I was due back to Ford tomorrow, and as much as we knew the chances were slim to get it extended again, we held onto hope. The phone went and Hannah tried the blag again but this time the call came from Prisoner Hater, Ford's Deputy Governor, Shirley. Hannah stated I was still feeling a little under the weather, just trying to chance her arm. Shirley blurted down the phone "If Daniel isn't back by 3pm tomorrow then he will be in breach of his license and we'll have to get the police involved." Talk about heavy handed, we didn't say I wasn't coming back, just putting the ball in their court.

Hannah snapped back saying about the restrictions of travel means that she can't drive me back and the train is meant only for keyworkers so how do she propose I get to Ford. Again, Shirley barked down the phone, "I don't care whether he infects everyone on the train, if he's not here by 3pm tomorrow, and we have taken all measures to look after everyone, he could face further charges for breach of licence". Hannah came off the phone crying in pure shock of the nonchalant response of the virus and also the disappointment of me going back.

We had to break the news gently to Tess as she had got used to having our family bond back, her dad being there and having the love of both parents, tomorrow that will all be turned upside down.

The day came, you go numb to have to deal with the reality of where you are heading, the worst part, knowing that the prison is currently in closed conditions. We have no idea when we will get a ROTL again, if ever, before the end of my sentence. Visits are currently closed too and what will happen when I get back, no doubt I will end up in quarantine, but to spend two extra weeks at home with my family, I'll take it.

I had to peel myself away from my girls as the water works started and I had to make the train. Southampton station, usually a hive of activity, was like a ghost town, it was dead. Not one person in sight or on the train apart from the conductor, I felt like a stowaway.

The tannoy on the train kept repeating on a loop, "This train is operating for key workers only, if you're not a keyworker, you're part of the problem, leave the train, go home, stay safe". Well, what are they going to do, send me to prison? Why I couldn't just be under house arrest and stay home baffles me, what if I did have it and now they want me to come back into the prison and infect everyone, and everyone on the train as Shirley so pleasantly put it.

Chapter 30. Prisons Didn't Take the Covid Seriously

The hour journey back to the prison went like a flash, and walking back in I took a deep breath and prepared myself for what I was to face with regard to the precautions the prison would take due to Covid-19.

I was secretly worried. I was fine, but how many other people who could have Coronavirus would be stood in Reception, how are they going to handle maintaining a safe distance, processing everyone in a small space, keeping everyone quarantined. I didn't want to get it thanks to the prison just throwing everyone in the same boat. Time to walk in and see what's in store.

I expected hospital like conditions and precautions, people in hazmat's and excessively spraying everything as we made our way back into the prison. I was even expected to be handed PPE on the way in to protect myself and others.

We were temperature checked and herded into Reception with about 15 others. Everyone was ushered into one waiting room, no protection and with all our belongings, this is disgusting, and they hadn't taken this seriously at all. If one of the 15 had genuinely got Covid, we have now all got it thanks to Dainton and the prison!

Not one officer was wearing any form of protection, as they stood chatting behind the Reception desk like it was a normal day. I took it upon myself to wait outside as I don't really fancy waiting in an incubation room with 15 other people. They called us in one at a time to get checked over by Healthcare (the only person sensible enough to wear head to toe PPE), have our property checked then taken into the prison. The lady in Healthcare did apologise for us being brought back in and let slip that it was against the Healthcare Department's advice which was interesting.

I waited last to be seen, which was lucky as all the people who had been seen, and who I thought had made their way back to their rooms, but everyone was locked in a holding cell together until we had all been seen, it's disgusting! There had been no attempt to protect me or anyone else, no duty of care at all especially during this pandemic, no precaution and no fucks given for themselves or me.

The officers were as giddy as could be as they lead us as a group to P1 and G1 billets which had been secluded off with metal fences that you would find at a concert. With a smirk on their faces, they had great pleasure in letting us know that we would all be quarantined for 14 days, lose our old rooms and will not be socialising with the rest of the prison until the 14 days are up.

All my belongings had been gathered from my old room and dumped in P1-07, and as I unpacked the bell went indicating it was exercise time. The whole prison was in lockdown too with no work, no ROTLs, no outside work and people only got to come out for 30 minutes of exercise at a time.

The news of our arrival had circulated round the prison and people gathered around the perimeter shouting for certain friends or people they knew had been away for the past 2 weeks. As I went outside for fresh air, I felt like the star attraction at a zoo. Everyone asking questions about who had it, who was in this makeshift cage and everyone's worried about all of us spreading it to the rest of the prison. People jeered as they walked by "Stay away, they've all got corona!". You could feel the bitterness in people who have all had their future ROTLs cancelled and we have just come back from an extended holiday does not sit well with people.

As I sat on my bed, surrounded by people that I didn't know on the billet, I felt like I did when I first got into prison, this felt like a new sentence all over again, it was an awful dark and lonely feeling with nothing to look forward to. Visits cancelled, ROTLs cancelled, work cancelled and being apart from my normal prison friends for at least 2 weeks minimum was horrible. Just kept thinking to myself, I'd have taken this for 2 weeks at home so suck it up!

News spread quickly that someone on C1, which was the medically vulnerable wing anyway, had come down with Coronavirus, followed by 3 officers who were all off work self-isolating after testing positive. It was inevitable, so many people in such a small environment and the officers did themselves no favours with the majority choosing not to wear PPE.

If not for themselves, as a cohort we were all isolating away from the general public so the only way it would penetrate Ford was from the outside of the prison, it's their own doing.

The days in quarantine dragged, I watched multiple box sets (including Prison Break, ironically), wrote multiple letters, prepared school worksheets for Tess, ate, slept and clock watched. All the food was brought directly to our billets to save us leaving the confines.

Just as we were coming to the end of our first week, someone else returned to the prison and, again with no precautions, he was dumped in the spare room we had in our billet. Our 14 days then reset; it was a crushing blow. I felt like I was back at Wandsworth again just passing the time lying on my bed. We got let out 8:30 till 9:30am then 5:45 till 6:15pm, the area we were segregated off to walk round took a whole 4 mins to do a full lap. I got bored of the walk after one day!

The death toll in total has now surpassed 17,000 and half the prison estates are now infected with Covid-19. I'm hearing of more and more cases inside Ford but they are trying to keep it under wraps. It's obvious, though, when a full medical team head to toe in PPE enter a certain billet, ambulances are called and then the room quarantined.

The pandemic is now becoming a pandemic of its own inside prisons and they can't just ignore it or keep it from being public knowledge anymore. The press keeps releasing articles of deaths in custody and how many cases there are in the HMPs.

A statement has just been released to all prisoners via a letter which indicates a Covid-19 Early Release Scheme is being implemented. The Ministry of Justice has confirmed that low-risk prisoners within 61 days of their release can be released under the new scheme on HDC. This measure is being taken to ease the pressure, reduce the spread of coronavirus and the extra strain on the NHS. Exclusions would be High Risk, no MAPPA, no violent or sexual crimes. I just hope it's still ongoing when I reach my 61 days remaining which is still about 4 months away. Fingers Crossed.

Officers Too Hot to wear PPE! As the figures worldwide skyrocket, I was getting more and more pissed off seeing the careless and unconcerned attitude of the officers who walked round, enjoying the free time as most prisoners were confined to their rooms, and wearing no PPE whatsoever.

I asked if there was a shortage of PPE within prisons and why no officers seemed to be wearing them. "No one can be arsed and its uncomfortable in this heat". No effort to protect prisoners from the virus coming into the prison at all.

We have been in lockdown for over a month now and finally I've been released from quarantine. I moved to C2, a few doors down to where Curtis moved throughout the shuffle around due to using the P1 and C1 billets for the caged Zoo.

People were a bit funny with me at first thinking that I was a Corona carrier but after a few days finally dropped the act. I moved into C2-12, it had only just been freshly painted, had 2 mattresses, curtains and a nice comfy armchair. I'd won the lottery with this room!

The virus was getting worse with 20,000 UK deaths now reported on TV, me and Curtis would watch the daily news briefing together every evening and the increase in cases is even echoed in here.

O2 Billet, the over 50's billet, had an elderly gentleman complain of breathing difficulties, was tested and taken to hospital due to having Coronavirus. Problem being, most of the billet rooms are double occupancy so you can see how quickly the virus can spread here.

The whole O2 billet had to also be isolated off like P1 and C1, more staff had also gone missing due to coming down with the virus which put more pressure on the existing staff with having to deliver meals, post and oversee a military-style watch of exercise to ensure people don't mingle with other parts of the prison.

Week 4 in lockdown, with no ROTLs or visits they have allowed us to have 45 minute sessions on our mobile phones in the Visits Hall. You had to book a week in advance, get your phone from the locker and sit in a designated chair which were in spaced out lines.

I had my first call with Hannah and Tess and they were that overwhelmed to see me, I barely got a hello before Tess couldn't speak anymore due to crying down the phone. As much as it was nice to see them after a month, it was so painful. You get used to being numb, a routine, learning to cope then seeing each other just resets it all.

Week 5 in lockdown, although they said they wouldn't do prison transfers to stop the spread, they have started receiving prison transfers again from places such as Lewes and Wandsworth, the prisons that were currently riddled with the virus. They have put them all in the G1 and G2 isolation billets for 14 days which was their way of curtailing the spread of the virus. It's well intentioned, yet the staff at Reception, officers now doing their induction and doing roll checks never bother wearing PPE so the whole concept is pretty pointless. The 2m distance rule doesn't apply here either, only when it suits.

Week 6 in lockdown, nearly 30,000 UK deaths reported on the news and we get two 1-hour exercise sessions a day which doesn't seem enough. Still, I am so thankful to be in open conditions and not closed like Wandsworth, the Bank Holiday weekends were bad enough. I've got 5 months left and I just keep hoping the early release scheme stays open long enough for me to be able to apply. No one's left here yet on the scheme, so it seems it's just a hoodwink to give the impression they care but there's no urgency in the matter.

Chapter 31. The Pantom Shitter

A lot of people in the prison who worked outside would use their mobile phones during the day so had no use for the prison phone. Now everyone is going a little stir crazy and boredom is taking hold, so the prison phone is an outlet and one of the only forms of communication to your loved ones

There's 18 of us on the landing all fighting to use the single phone, and there is now an unofficial queuing system where you have to let the person know you're waiting; firstly, to try and hurry them up and secondly, so no-one else jumps in as soon as they are finished. It's causing a lot of heated arguments and especially for those who like a long phone call. I've sometimes waited an hour to get to the phone. It's only a small booth and it can stink of body odour and sweat by the time someone's finished in there.

I'm also so cautious using the phone, with people's spittle and them coughing, sneezing and breathing down the handset and I've now got to go and pick it up to call home. It's quite grim.

With everyone being forced to eat the awful prison food, not working outside the prison and the only thing to do is sleep and eat, the toilets on the wing are taking a battering. They are filthy in the best of times but the whole of C2 landing have started an internal investigation to try and find out who the Phantom Shitter is.

Each morning someone dumps a log the size of King Kong's finger in the toilet and leaves it there proudly to bask all day. It has got quite amusing to hear someone shout at 9am every morning down the hallway in disgust when they see the present that faced them when they went to use the facilities.

I'm so glad I'm in the main block now rather than the billets. With the frustration of being banged up together, the billets have issues daily with violence, drugs and alcohol. The officers have stopped doing room searches and drug tests due to Coronavirus, so the residents are taking full advantage. The virus is also taking hold of the prison. Q1, C1, G1, G2 and O2 are now all quarantined due to outbreaks of Covid-19. It's no surprise when another ambulance turns up at the prison to take a victim away from M billet after a stabbing due to a gang related argument, and another 4 people got shipped out. The next day, exactly the same happened again but on K billet. Seeing ambulances arrive at the gate is a daily occurrence now, whether its due to violence or coronavirus.

Week 8 of lockdown, 33,000 deaths reported in the UK. I feel like I'm going insane with the same mundane routine, solitary confinement conditions and dealing with the same inconsiderate people, battling for the phones, showers and even to get a free toilet. The Phantom Shitter is still at large and not been identified.

Phone calls home are tough, and when I've had a bad day, I call home to get support from my wife. Then when she's had a bad day, especially as Tess is now off school due to school closures and she's got Tess 24/7. When I call, she wants to unload so in the end I have to be strong to support her and come off the phone feeling worse than when I called.

The lockdown is making prisoners irritable and most have reached boiling point with one another. The tension, confined space, atmosphere, contraband and general boredom is creating a hostile environment which the prison can't control with it still being open conditions (the only difference being, the gate is now shut). The 3rd stabbing this week has just been reported, where tweezers bought from the Canteen were used to stab someone in the face. The whole prison has a scent of weed wherever you walk. They have lost control.

Week 9 of lockdown, 37,500 UK deaths reported on the news tonight. America has just surpassed 100,000 and the number of cases reported worldwide is through the roof. When food gets delivered to the wing it's like a hoard of zombies, and people have started queuing down the wing hallway to ensure they get first takings. Like Wandsworth, chicken day or burger day, the delivery is usually short and those at the back miss out and end up having a salad or sandwich as an alternative.

Although the place is meant to be sanitary to stop the spread of the virus, the prison couldn't be filthier. Overflowing bins, shit smeared in every toilet, showers are flooded, the landing kitchen littered in food waste and no soap for the sinks. It's hot too, with the temperature now over 23 degrees, and the officers are all huddled together out the front of A Wing office, wearing no PPE, laughing, joking and chatting the day away with no social distancing at all.

The highlight of the week was that a prisoner who was still allowed across the road as they worked in the Recycling Department of the prison got shipped out today. He got caught in the act in the prison car park with a prostitute that he had arranged using a smuggled in mobile phone. Got taken down the block and shipped out. That's the only issue with doing nothing, idle hands do the devil's work. I guess being sex starved for 2 months, the man had needs and that itch needed to be scratched!

Week 11 of lockdown

40,000 UK deaths and officers have given up on their duty of care. The CMs don't even come out of their office anymore, the Deputy Governor who demanded I came back and assured me it's safe here is at home self-isolating, and we have had 60 prisoners from other prisons come here since the start of lockdown.

Staff still choose not to wear PPE, post is getting beyond a joke and is days, sometimes weeks, late, apps are going missing and only 7 in total have made it out on the Early Release Scheme so far!

Hannah has been pestering my Probation Officer like a dog with a bone and today we had some great news. After stringent checks for things like ROTL breaches, nickings, risk, and backing of my Offender Manager, "I'VE MADE THE LIST," Hannah shouted down the phone to me today with glee! My release date is Oct 2020, which means I'd be out in August 2020 which makes a world of difference. Just knowing I'm on the list is an overwhelming feeling! Just hope it doesn't get pulled in the meantime.

Want an Ocado delivery during lockdown? Just pay a prison officer! The food portions have got so small that the meals feel like snacks, laundry has stopped as the machines have broken with the increasing amount of washing that needs to be done, and the Canteen deliveries are running dry. Most popular items are now no longer available or limited to one item per prisoner.

Those officers who usually get paid to be a drug mule or bring in other items such as phones, are now adapting with the change of time. A prime example; an old London gangster that resides on F Wing has extremely deep pockets. After working in the Gym, he got friendly with and turned one of the Gym screws into his own little prison Ocado delivery service. For a healthy monthly fee, he is delivered steaks, bacon, a nice selection of cheeses, fresh fruit, a bakery selection and just fell short of a nice bottle of Champagne to wash it all down. There were two fridges on F Wing and when Curtis and I went to visit, he proudly showed us the one he had commandeered, which was brimming with goods. He kindly offered us some cheese, but I'd have much preferred a bacon sandwich!

More people are using the mobile phone service now in the Visits Hall. You're now lucky to get one a week and people get there so early to queue outside to get maximum time on their phone that by the time the officers get you checked in and seated it's less than an hour. I never thought in my life I'd have to queue to use my own mobile phone. Getting access to my mobile also allowed me to order a small wooden Love frame and a pair of earrings as a surprise for our 5th wedding anniversary.

Week 14 in lockdown 42,000 deaths in the UK and 4 months until my release, with 8 weeks until I could potentially get released on the Early Release Scheme. I never hold out much hope as I don't like to build myself up for a downfall. Only 9 people so far have left from Ford, with only 250 from the total prison estate, which shows me that HMP aren't keen to release people on the scheme.

It's Curtis' 56th birthday tomorrow. I've stocked up over the weeks on items from the Canteen. Kenco coffee, Marmite portions, honey, hazelnut chocolate spread, cream soda, Dime, Twix, Mars and a Snickers. I've grabbed a cardboard box from the officers' office and decorated it to create a makeshift hamper. Just a little token gesture to show my appreciation for having a great, close friend to share this prison journey with.

Time feels like it's stood still. Each day drags and it's mentally challenging feeling isolated and cut-off from the world and my loved ones. Me and Curtis have managed to get through 4 series of Blacklist to pass the evenings. Even though we are meant to stick to our own Wings, during the day I make my way to my friend Brynn's on D Wing and we play Xbox and watch movies which he has downloaded using his iPhone which he keeps in his room. We have also started working out together with makeshift weights of bottles of water in a bag for life. The things we do to pass the time!

Due to hunger, we are having to combine the meat we get from the dinners with other items and ingredients to feel fuller for longer such as rice, pasta and egg noodles.

By the time we get around to eating in the evening and settling in to binge watch a boxset, our guts are rejecting the Chinese imported reconstructed, mechanically reclaimed cat and dog meat. It does allow for some light comedy, like men behaving badly. As we sit, we take it in turns to unearth a silent but deadly fart and wait in anticipation as it reaches the other person's nostrils. I'm terrible at the game and end up smelling it first and chuckling to myself as I keep an eye on Curtis waiting for that exact moment it smacks him in the face. When he starts tasting it, I'm sat with streams of tears coming down my face in pure immaturity and humour watching as Curtis starts making wretching gagging noises.

Week 16 in lockdown, 43,000 UK deaths. Restaurants and shops are just about to re-open and the 2m rule is about to be reduced to 1m; however, the prison is to remain as it is, in lockdown. The mental health of prisoners is declining with the more time in solitary lockdown increases. There is more self-harming, more suicides and more drug taking than ever. If we were animals, the RSPCA would have intervened by now.

My stomach has stopped processing the prison food and I've been bunged up for 5 days. I feel so rough. I've tried orange juice, cod liver oil, exercise and the strongest coffee known to man but no movement. I can get hold of an iPhone or weed instantly but trying to get my hands on a diuretic is like getting gold dust.

Week 18 in lockdown, 44,000 deaths in the UK. Only 10 men have left Ford so far on the Early Release Scheme. All you seem to hear on the phones round the prison is arguments and many relationships have gone to shit from not seeing their loved ones. It's hard as well with not having anything to say on the phone. You want to check in, but nothing has happened with my day that is any different from yesterday and all my family have been able to do is stay at home.

I was speaking to a young drug dealer today who had got his hands on a mobile since arriving at the beginning of lockdown. He has made £20K in under 4 months from arranging delivery and collection of a selection of drugs. It seems a quick and easy way to make money, so no wonder so many people are in prison for drug dealing.

Only one more month until I should be signing my paperwork which you get 2 weeks before your early release date and it couldn't come sooner. There are rumours that the scheme may stop soon as lockdown is eased in the UK, and I'm getting nervy with it been so close yet so far.

Today's food was a Chicken Kiev which looked like it was stood on and grey inside. It came with 5 wedges, that was it. The wedges were so dehydrated that I could have snapped them; I've never eaten so much cereal to try and curb the hunger.

20 Weeks in isolation. Curtis had a knock on the door today, his release date is about 10 days before mine. It was the head of OMU and he was required to go down to Reception to sign his Early Release Scheme paperwork. This means that he will be out of the prison in 2 weeks' time. I was so happy for him and it just lifted our spirits to show it was still working and it shouldn't be long until I sign my own. The end is near.

There's a bad batch of ketamine that's been going around the prison, and so many people have been taken to hospital from being knocked unresponsive. The number of things coming over the fence is comical; they even stopped £250 worth of food coming over last night so the officers on the night shift must have had a right feast!

Chapter 32. IVE SIGNED MY EARLY RELEASE

80 days before my actual release date, I'm sat on the bed in the morning and get a knock at the door. I rushed to open it with an inkling that it might be an officer about my paperwork.

It was a female OS (Offender Supervisor) and she said that I'm required at Reception with regard to my Early Release Scheme. I rushed down there as quick as my feet would take me. The lady who administered the paperwork for the scheme at Ford was sat there waiting for me with a pen ready and all she required was for me to enter the address for me to be released to and to sign the documents.

I floated back to the wing and couldn't punch the number into the phone quick enough to call home and relay the good news to Hannah. That means in 2 weeks' time I will be out of here, albeit on tag, but I'm no longer in prison. My prison journey is over!

11th August, Curtis and I are having a coffee in his room when there's a knock on the door. It was the head of OMU again, and he tells Curtis everything is approved, signed off and he will be leaving the prison on Thursday.

We had spent the best part of 2 years 4 months together, shared a mound of experiences, good and bad, and since being at Ford had spent every evening together watching the worst films in the world. As excruciating as the 2 hours to get to the end of a bad film was, we did it together and to pass the time.

That pretty much sums up our prison journey together. As boring, pointless, lonely and tedious as it was, we got through it together, endured it together and like a bad film, we would laugh at how bad or awful it was just to get through it to the end. It feels like half of me is leaving the prison on Thursday.

13th August. 2pm came, which meant it was Curtis' time to finally leave the prison. Downing his last coffee with a shaking hand (you could see he was nervous/excited to get out) he grabbed the bags and boxes which contained all his items, we walked out of his room together and it felt surreal. We would never be going back into that room again to watch films, chat, when I wake in the morning, that chapter is over.

It felt slightly like a breakup as I acted like a concierge and aided him with his luggage to Reception whilst everyone shook his hand and wished him well as we went.

I congratulated him at the door to Reception, gave him a manly "Well done, mate" hug like our final goodbye and as I walked away, like a sap I shouted, "Miss you already" in a joking, but truthful, way. The remainder of my sentence, I'd have to do alone.

As I made my way back to the Wing with a tear in my eye, my new next-door neighbour was decorating his cell. Warren's a big tubby guy, goldfish bowl glasses, the same guy that disemboweled his boyfriend, I thought he was being sincere when he stopped me in the hallway and said, "You're going to miss him aren't you?" as he knew we had been friends throughout Ford. In jest, I replied, "Yeah, I'm going to cry into my pillow". I didn't expect the reply I got, "Well I've got a big enough bed for 2 tonight and I've got a lot of energy!". I just laughed and said cheers for the support warren, I'll be round at 8 as I entered my room and flicked the door lock behind me. I hope he knew I was only joking and he doesn't expect me at 8. If there is a knock on the door tonight, I will refuse to open it!

Wednesday 19th August 2020. It's been a week since Curtis has left and I've spent more time with Brynn during the days. I've mentally checked out of this place already and struggle to deal with people's habits, banter and comments. Everyone knows I signed my paperwork and they feel the need to constantly say "You Still here?" It's getting grating.

A shock to everyone. An emergency meeting was held in the prison dinner hall. The Governor gave an NTC (Notice to Community) which absolutely flattened me. "The Early Release Scheme is to cease on the 28th of August 2020 due to never fulfilling its commitment and due to the decline in Covid-19 Cases". It wasn't just me that felt the affect, the prison went into meltdown as that's the only hope people were holding onto.

It's just my luck they decide to cancel the scheme so close to the date when I'm due out. It will just be my luck that my confirmation doesn't come through in time before the 28th of August and I'll end up serving my last 2 months.

CHAPTER 33. IM GOING HOME!

I've already reached my 61 days and I've been chasing everyone, Probation, my OS, Head of OMU and the lady that takes care of the Early Release Scheme, all to no avail. I'm getting nervous.

As I sat and had my pigeon-sized purple chicken leg for lunch, a knock at my door, but luckily it wasn't Warren. "Mr Hockey, the Gov from OMU just called, you're all confirmed for early release 2pm tomorrow". I punched the air and had to stop myself from repeating "YES, YES, YES".

My admirer, Warren, heard the commotion and came in to shake my hand and give me well wishes which was nicer than his last sexual predatory comments. I started to bin old clothes, take down pictures and had to keep stopping as the reality and excitement overcame me.

This time tomorrow I won't be here, I'll be home! I'm absolutely buzzing. I felt like I'd won the lottery and called my girls who screamed down the phone. I went back to my room and was on cloud 9.

I hardly slept a wink, and had a million visitors at the door as the news of my departure spread. Most weren't there to wish me well; they were trying to get their hands on different items in my room before I left and the room got ravaged after I'd gone. Chair, plate, fan, cupboard, rug, bedding, DVD player, the room was pretty bare by the time I got to sleep. I just hope I do leave tomorrow!

The next morning, I sat with Brynn and we chatted about time spent together, the days trying to complete levels on the Xbox and experiences shared together. About 1:45, like Curtis, I made my way to Reception and Brynn helped me carry my items. The Wing all came to their doors to wave me goodbye and I said my final farewells to Brynn before making my way into Reception.

Some of the officers who I'd worked with throughout my time in Induction were behind the Reception desk so the paperwork went as smoothly as possible and they were pleased to see me finally being released. The only thing left to do was to have my HDC tag fitted.

My heart did start skipping a beat when the bloke was nowhere to be seen. Things weren't helped by the fact the officers said he was usually on time and there before the prisoner normally gets to Reception. He finally arrived at 2:15, to my relief. A small black box with a rubber strap was attached to my left ankle and that was it, I'm ready to go.

As I walked out the gates, I handed my paperwork to the gatehouse and my time inside was over. It didn't feel real, as I turned the corner, Tess, Hannah and my mother were waiting for me on the pavement.

Tess ran at full pelt and jumped into my arms, I just dropped everything I was carrying and time stopped. I've gained my life back, I'm a dad again, as I shimmied my way, with Tess still clinging, towards my wife. She threw her arms round me and we shouted "It's over, ITS OVER!" She was crying with pure joy, and I was completely bewildered, in a daze, it didn't feel real as mum was next to embrace my new freedom.

We put all my things into the car, I sat in the back with Tess and she did nothing but stare at me intensely and Hannah, beaming from ear to ear said, "Let's go home".

Mum started the engine, I just looked one final time at the place that I'd called home for the past 19 months and as it faded into the distance we cheered, celebrated and were in total awe that, like many ROTLs previously, we were on our way home. The difference being this time I'm not going back. EVER! This awful, tragic, unbelievable and painful time of my life is finally over, I'm finally back with my lovely, beautiful and supportive family.

Thank you for taking the time to read my story.
Just remember..

"if you're going through hell, keep going"
Winston Churchill

It may seem like it now, but the tough times in your life won't last forever

Printed in Great Britain
by Amazon